Purpose Renaissance

in an AI Driven World

SANTHOSH ASIR

Focus on your unique God given purpose and destiny will happen

INDIA · SINGAPORE · MALAYSIA

ISBN
Paperback 979-8-89632-838-4
Hardcase 979-8-89673-756-8

I've had the privilege of reading numerous books on purpose and meaning, but Purpose Renaissance: in an AI driven world stands out for its unique blend of spiritual insight, practical wisdom, and real-world application. What resonated with me most was the way Santhosh seamlessly weaves together timeless principles and contemporary examples to create a compelling narrative that is both inspiring and empowering.

As a business leader, I've seen firsthand the transformative impact that a sense of purpose can have on individuals, teams, and organizations. This book offers a powerful framework for discovering and living out one's purpose, and I highly recommend it to anyone seeking to make a meaningful difference in their personal, professional lives and also for societal transformation.

Dennison John,
Managing Director, SAP Labs Latin America
Rio Grande do Sul, Brazil / Monterrey, Mexico

I take this opportunity to thank and appreciate Mr. Santhosh for writing this book "Purpose Renaissance: in an AI Driven World!" He has written this book taking into consideration the Divine Purpose of human life and the negative influence of AI that tries to reshape human life in every area of human existence. AI is shifting the ideas of human potential, creativity and nature of work! Purpose of life is a Divine calling; every individual is unique, and they should understand the purpose of life. It calls for self-cognition, self-awareness, self-discovery and self-definition from God's perspective! Only God can give humans clarity about the purpose of life! AI appears to simulate human intelligence. God has created humans as "creative thinkers and thoughtful creators! AI is artificial and it can never help humans to fulfil the purpose of life designated by God! I believe that this book will enhance value inculcation and character formation in individuals ushering in social transformation!

With love and prayers,
Rev. Dr. Y. Rajadhas, M.Sc., B.D., M.Th., D.Min., Ph.D.
Former HOD, Department of Personality Development, Karunya University
Former Principal, HBI, Chennai, India

This book could be read with profit by any older teenager or young adult, whether they have a faith or not; the warm encouragement to think for oneself, explore one's own interests and gifts and find a purpose to give life meaning is universally applicable. The author does not hesitate to venture onto controversial territory and express his own views, especially on gender identification and roles, but this can be seen as a stimulus to discussion and debate. There are two particularly interesting chapters on the current and future possibilities of Artificial Intelligence, about which the author is clearly knowledgeable, and he urges his readers to take seriously the philosophical and ethical problems which are posed by different forms of A.I. - a message which people of all ages need to hear.

Rachel Stuchbury,
Lay Reader, Church of England, West London, UK

Santhosh has written a profoundly insightful and timely book that serves as a guide for anyone seeking to discover their purpose in an age dominated by artificial intelligence. As we navigate the uncharted territories of an AI-driven world, this book offers a compelling roadmap for reclaiming our success, reigniting our passions, and redefining our sense of purpose.

By mastering the principles explored in this book, readers will be empowered to transcend the limitations of a rapidly changing world and unlock a life of purpose, fulfilment, and happiness. A must-read for anyone seeking to thrive in the AI age and leave a lasting impact on the world.

Dr. E.M. Epongo, Ph.D.
Founder & President of Rebuilding a New Africa
Athens, Greece

I wholeheartedly recommend the book, 'Purpose Renaissance: in an AI-Driven World'. This thought-provoking and insightful work is a testament of dedication to exploring the complexities of our rapidly changing world. As a parent, it has been incredible to witness my Son's growth and passion for understanding the intersection of humanity and technology. His unique perspective and meticulous research has resulted in a book that is both informative and inspiring. But what I am most proud of is not just the intellectual curiosity, but also the sincerity and commitment to making a positive impact. From childhood Santhosh has always demonstrated a genuine desire to help others and make the world a better place. 'Purpose Renaissance in an AI-Driven World' is more than just a book - it's a call to action, urging readers to rethink their values, passions, and contributions in a world where artificial intelligence is increasingly prevalent. This work will challenge your assumptions, spark meaningful reflections, and empower you to discover your purpose in this new era.

I am honoured to endorse this remarkable book and invite you to join the conversation. Read 'Purpose Renaissance : in an AI-Driven World' and discover the transformative power of purpose in a world of rapid change."

Dr. R. Asir, M.Sc., Ph.D.

Former Scientist, ICAR, Govt., of India.

Coimbatore, India

Dedication

To the young leaders and next generation world changers who are eager to make their mark and leave a lasting impact. This book is dedicated to you. May it fuel your passion, ignite your purpose and guide you on your journey to making a meaningful difference in the world.

&

This book is dedicated to my loving parents, Dr. R. Asir, M.Sc., Ph.D., and Mrs. G. Nesamani, who taught me the value of learning and the importance of living with purpose. Your endless love and sacrifices have made this book a reality. I am deeply grateful for everything you have done for me, and I thank God for the chance to honor you both through this dedication. I also thank God for His guidance and the inspiration He provided as I wrote this book, and for the gift of life, love, and purpose that has shaped every page.

Contents

Foreword

As we navigate the uncharted waters of the 21st century, Santhosh Asir's book, [Purpose Renaissance: in an AI Driven World], emerges as a beacon of hope, wisdom, and insight. This inspiring work tackles the most pressing questions of our time, inviting readers to embark on a profound journey of self-discovery, exploration, and transformation.

In an era where artificial intelligence, automation, and technological advancements are redefining the very fabric of our society, Santhosh boldly challenges us to rethink our assumptions about purpose, identity, human fulfilment, and what it means to be alive. With unflinching honesty, vulnerability, and a deep understanding of the human condition, Santhosh guides us through the complexities of our times, offering a nuanced and insightful exploration of the human experience.

Throughout these pages he masterfully weaves together a rich tapestry of ideas, drawing from a wide range of disciplines, including Technology, philosophy, psychology, sociology, and theology. The result is a work that is both deeply personal and universally relevant, speaking to readers from all walks of life.

One of the most significant contributions of this book is its ability to inspire readers to think critically about the world around them, to question their assumptions, and to seek out new possibilities. The book is infused with a sense of hope, optimism, and urgency, encouraging readers to take action, to make a difference, and to leave a lasting legacy.

I firmly believe this book has the potential to transform lives, communities, and societies. Santhosh's courage, wisdom, and dedication to exploring the most pressing questions of our time are a testament to the power of the human spirit. This book is a must-read for anyone seeking to navigate the challenges and opportunities of our rapidly changing world.

Dr.A.E. Muthunayagam M.E., Ph.D.
Former Chairman, Board of Governors-IIT Madras,
Former Secretary to Govt., of India

Endorsement

I am delighted to wholeheartedly recommend "Purpose Renaissance: in an AI-Driven World" by Mr. Santhosh Asir. This remarkable book is a clarion call to rediscover our true purpose and values in a world increasingly dominated by artificial intelligence.

With unflinching honesty and compassion, the author tackles some of the most pressing issues of our time, including the distortions of false feminism, the dangers of extremism, and the persistent scourge of caste divides. Through a nuanced exploration of self-discovery, passion, and values, the author offers a powerful antidote to the dehumanizing forces that threaten our world.

This book is a must-read for anyone seeking to navigate the complexities of our AI-driven world with integrity, wisdom, and hope. It is a call to awaken to our true purpose and to live with intention, compassion, and courage.

I highly recommend "Purpose Renaissance: in an AI-Driven World" to anyone seeking a thought-provoking and inspiring read.

With my warmest recommendations,
Rt. Rev. Sharma Nithiyanandham B.D., M.Th.
Bishop in Vellore &
Bishop in Charge, Madras Diocese

Acknowledgements

As I pen these words of acknowledgement, I am overwhelmed with gratitude and humility. Firstly, I thank God who helped me turn my dreams into reality. I would like to express my sincere and heartfelt thanks to the legendary visionaries, esteemed spiritual leaders, educational experts and distinguished industry leaders who have played a significant role in shaping this journey. To **Dr. A.E. Muthunayagam**, former Secretary to Govt of India. The legendary Chief Architect and Father of Rocket Propulsion Technology in India's space program (ISRO), I am forever grateful for your generosity in writing the foreword for this book. Your endorsement is a testament to your commitment to support young talent and authors like me. To **Rt. Rev. Sharma Nithiyanandham**, Bishop of Vellore and Bishop In charge, Madras Diocese, I am deeply thankful for immediately accepting to endorse this book and for your spiritual guidance and blessings. I've always been inspired by your humility and leadership style. Your endorsement is a reminder of the power of simplicity, faith and determination. To **Dr. Emmanuel Epongo**, Founder of Rebuilding Africa, your work on transforming Africa through decentralization is truly visionary. I salute your tireless efforts to rebuild and empower communities by being a change agent. Your recommendation is a testament of our shared understanding of Kingdom purpose and kingdom values. To **Rev.Y. Rajadhas**, a distinguished theologian of uncommon depth and nuance. I sincerely thank your encouragement and recommendation. To **Rachel and Ian Stuchbury**, Lay Readers from the church of England, West London for reading the complete manuscript and giving valuable and insightful suggestions. It is a privilege to receive the endorsement from such accomplished people like you. To **John Dennison**, Managing Director of SAP Labs, Latin America. I've always been inspired by your exceptional shrewdness and leadership style which has taken the organization under your leadership to #1 GPTW in Latin America. I'm honored and grateful for your recommendation of the book in your busy schedule. I would also like to express my heartfelt gratitude to my loving family, who have been my rock, my inspiration, and my joy.

To my wonderful wife, **Sujitha**. Your unwavering love, support, and patience have been my guiding force. To my precious children, **Shannon** and **Shiphra**, you are the stars that light up my life. Your innocence, curiosity, and enthusiasm have taught me the value of wonder and awe. To my parents, **Dr. R. Asir** and **Mrs. G. Nesamani**, I owe a debt of gratitude for your selfless love, guidance, and sacrifices. You have instilled in me the values of hard work, integrity, and compassion. To my brother **Prince** and **Sowmya Prince**, you are my confidants. Your love, support, and camaraderie have been a constant source of strength and inspiration. To my uncle Anand, thanks for the constant support.

Thank you all for being part of this journey. Your love, support, and encouragement have made this book possible.

Santhosh
Feltham, West London
08/12/2024

Introduction

We are living in a time of major change. As we move through 2024 and beyond, rapid advancements in technology, especially in artificial intelligence (AI), are reshaping almost every part of our lives, from how we communicate and work to how we learn and interact with the world. The use of AI in our daily lives is more than just new technology; it's shifting our ideas of human potential, creativity, and even the nature of work.

Technological Advancements

The speed of change today is unlike anything we've seen before. AI, machine learning, and automation are bringing incredible efficiencies and new capabilities, pushing industries to evolve fast. Businesses now use data to make quick, informed decisions, and this shift is changing the roles and skills needed in the workforce. With technologies like AI, robotics, and the Internet of Things (IoT) connecting, our way of living and working is fundamentally changing.

Societal and Ethical Challenges

These advancements raise important ethical questions. As AI becomes a part of decision-making in areas like healthcare, finance, and law enforcement, we face questions about responsibility, transparency, and fairness. Now is the time to think critically about how we use technology, protect privacy, and consider its impact on all communities. This shift urges us to reconsider our values and ensure that technology truly benefits humanity.

Rethinking Human Potential

This era of change is also leading us to rethink what it means to be human. The line between human abilities and AI is becoming less clear, which prompts us to look closely at qualities that define us, like creativity, empathy, and moral judgment. While AI can enhance some of our skills, it's our human traits—like intuition and ethics—that are essential. As we go forward, it's crucial to focus on these traits, making sure they guide our progress.

Facing Change with Confidence

To handle these changes, we need to build skills and flexibility. Adapting to this rapid shift means preparing individuals for an AI-driven world through education and community support. By encouraging collaboration and flexibility, we can tackle the challenges ahead and make the most of technology's benefits for society.

The importance of this era can't be overstated. As we go through these changes, we're not just observers; we're shaping a future where technology and humanity work together. By moving forward with purpose and a sense of responsibility, we can build a society that values both innovation and the well-being of individuals and communities. This is our chance to guide progress in a way that lifts up and inspires all of humanity.

In a world where machines are becoming smarter every day, we are faced with a question that has been around for ages: What is our purpose? As artificial intelligence (AI) reshapes how we live, work, and think, the search for meaning feels more important than ever.

For hundreds of years, humans have turned to philosophy, religion, and science to understand their place in the world. Now, with AI rapidly evolving, many of us are left wondering if those old ideas of purpose still hold true. The rise of intelligent machines has shaken our traditional understanding, making us question whether we can still find meaning in a world where technology seems to be taking over.

Some people believe that purpose is something we create ourselves through our achievements. But what if that idea is incomplete?

> *"Purpose is not human ingenuity, but divine design."*
>
> – Santhosh

This thought challenges us to look beyond the technology that surrounds us and dive deeper into the meaning of our lives. It suggests that our purpose isn't something we invent, but something we discover—a design created for us from the very beginning and already woven into our lives by divine intention.

In a world focused on personal success and constant change, it's important to remember that our true purpose is more than our skills and achievements. While we often work hard to make our own paths, our purpose is guided by a bigger plan, one that brings us closer to real fulfillment. This helps us pause and see that there is meaning beyond what we accomplish.

The purpose is not just something that happens by chance or from our own efforts. It is a gift from a higher power, shaping our experiences, relationships, and goals. Like an artist creating a painting with care, our lives are shaped with a purpose that connects us to a larger story. When we recognize this, we see ourselves as part of something bigger, finding meaning in the journey itself, not only in the end results.

When we understand that purpose is not only about what we create, we gain a clearer view of our place in the world. Modern life often pushes us to focus on success and status, but these can leave us feeling empty. Seeing purpose as part of a greater plan lets us align our goals with something deeper, bringing a sense of peace and connection. It reminds us that we are not alone in our search for meaning; we are part of a larger design, with a creator who sees our potential.

Seeing purpose in this way encourages us to live with intention and gratitude. It leads us to find guidance in the spiritual truths that speak to us, allowing our lives to grow within this larger plan. By trusting in this wisdom, we learn that true purpose is about more than our achievements; it is also about who we become along the way. Purpose becomes a journey of self-discovery and connection to something far greater than ourselves.

As we navigate this AI-driven world, we need to ask ourselves: What makes us different from machines? What gives our lives significance? In this book, we will explore these questions and more, focusing on the intersection of purpose, technology, and faith. We will cover topics like:

- The limits of finding purpose in human achievements alone
- The power of divine design and how it transforms how we see life
- Practical steps to discover your true purpose
- Providing solutions for urgent and critical problems in a technology-driven world.

This book is here to guide you on your journey to rediscover your unique God given purpose in a world where machines may be smart, but the human soul remains priceless.

As we move forward together, consider these questions:

- What if your purpose isn't something you create but something you are meant to find?
- Could technology help you discover your purpose instead of taking it away?
- Is your purpose rooted in something deeper than human creativity?

Join me as we explore what it means to live with purpose in this ever-changing, AI-driven world.

'Purpose is not a result of our own making; it is a gift from a higher power, guiding us toward our true calling'

CHAPTER

1 The Last Generation of Innocence

'Focus on your unique God-given purpose and destiny will happen'

- Santhosh

Ours is the last generation who were innocent. Think of our grandmothers. They grew up in a time when life was simpler. They didn't have the internet or smartphones showing them everything all the time. They lived their lives with a certain innocence, untouched by the complexities we face today.

Our mothers found joy in simple things. A family meal, a walk in the park, a good book. They didn't need the latest gadgets or social media likes to feel good about themselves. They were happy because they didn't have to deal with so many choices and comparisons.

In those days, life had a certain purity. They weren't always told how to look, what to buy, or how to live, they didn't let too many voices influence them. They just listened to their hearts and did their own thing.

Today, we are always connected, always online. We see everything, hear everything, and sometimes, it's too much. We're the last generation who remembers what it was like to live without all this constant noise. The last ones to experience true innocence before the world changed so much.

But what does this mean for us? How can we find that same sense of contentment in a world that never stops? How do we identify what truly makes us come alive? Let's start with identifying your passion.

As I stood at the meeting point of Argentina, Brazil, and Paraguay, with the sound of Iguazu Falls in the distance, I felt amazed by how big the world is. But even as I took in the beauty around me, one question kept coming to my mind: What is our purpose? Does God have a purpose for each of us?

Reflecting on my travels, from the streets of Buenos Aires to the historic Westminster Abbey, and the skyline of Shanghai, I realized that purpose is something that crosses all cultures and places.

In 2008 in Argentina, I was moved by the natural beauty and the friendly people. During quiet moments, I found myself thinking about what drives us as humans to explore, create, and connect. These moments made me reflect on the deeper meaning behind what we do.

In 2010 in Shanghai, where old traditions blended with new changes, I reflected on how one can find purpose in an ever-changing world. Every culture offers its own understanding of purpose, but I believe it's God's design that gives our lives the deepest sense of meaning.

During my visit to Westminster Abbey in 2024, I saw how purpose had shaped the lives of great people like Newton, Darwin, and Dickens. Their work continues to influence the world today, showing how a strong sense of purpose can leave a lasting impact.

Through all these experiences, I've learned that purpose is something everyone searches for, no matter where they come from. It's personal to each of us, yet connected to something greater that gives our lives true meaning.

I believe today's generation may be the last to experience real innocence. In a world shaped by artificial intelligence, "the last generation of innocence" suggests that today's young people may be the final group to know a world mostly free from the impact of AI. They stand on the edge of a new era, where their views on life, relationships, and creativity might change in ways we can't fully predict.

As AI continues to grow, the natural curiosity and imagination of young people face new challenges. Children today are surrounded by AI-driven technology. From social media algorithms that influence what they see to virtual assistants that shape their daily lives, this constant exposure to AI makes it harder for them to connect with the world as it is. Reality often feels mixed with artificial influences.

This constant presence of AI brings up questions that earlier generations never faced. Issues like data privacy, tracking, and deepfakes make us rethink trust and what is real. Young people, as they start to understand these issues, may lose some of the innocence that comes from seeing the world simply. Instead of spending these years only playing and exploring, they now have to understand and question the technology around them.

This shift makes us think about how to protect childhood in a world full of AI. It calls on parents, teachers, and leaders to create spaces where children can use technology safely while also building thinking skills and emotional awareness. By creating spaces where children can connect with each other and with nature, we can help keep their curiosity and creativity alive as technology grows.

In this time of AI, "the last generation of innocence" reminds us to balance new technology with what makes us human. As we move into a world that relies more on machines, we need to protect the unique views and creativity of today's youth. By understanding how AI affects their growth, we can work toward a balance that respects their innocence and prepares them for the future.

Your purpose is the reason for your existence, the foundation that guides your life. It shapes your actions and decisions. Purpose often comes from your values, the things you care about, your passions, and the strengths that make you who you are.

Purpose is discovered through soul-searching, not solely created by human effort or following frameworks. There is a divine involvement in one's unique purpose.

We can't create meaning and purpose in one's life through human effort alone. We need to discover our unique God-given purpose.

Purpose is not just about self-determination or following a framework; it's about discovering why God created you and understanding how He has placed desires and dreams within you.

Dreams

Dreams are the God-given desires that inspire and motivate you. These are the things that excite you and give you something to look forward to. Your dreams come from your purpose and help you move in the direction you want your life to take.

Vision

A vision is a clear idea of what you want your future to look like. It gives you focus and helps you see the life you want to create. Vision guides you by showing what success means for you, based on your dreams and purpose.

Destiny

Destiny is the overall plan God has for your life. It includes the different experiences, roles, and responsibilities you will take on throughout your journey. Your destiny is bigger than individual moments, it's the complete picture of your life's purpose.

Calling

A calling is a specific task or role that God wants you to fulfill. It is often connected to your strengths and passions and is a way for you to make a meaningful impact in the world. Your calling is something that feels uniquely yours, a role that makes use of your abilities in a special way.

Practical Applications

Reflect on Your Purpose: Spend time thinking about your purpose, dreams, vision, mission, destiny, and calling. Each of these is connected and plays a role in guiding your life.

Identify Overlaps: Find where your purpose, vision, and calling come together. These are key areas where you can focus your efforts.

Seek Clarity: Reflect or pray for understanding of your specific calling and how it fits within the bigger picture of your life.

Identifying Your Passion

Your purpose is a divine assignment written on your heart by the hand of God himself.

Finding your passion is like discovering a hidden part of yourself. It's that thing that makes you feel excited and alive. For some, it might be art, music, or writing. For others, it might be helping people, solving problems, or exploring new ideas.

Passion is not just a hobby or an interest. It's something deeper that gives your life meaning. It's what you love to do, even if no one is watching. It's what makes you lose track of time because you're so engaged in it.

Think about the times when you felt happiest and most fulfilled. What were you doing? Who were you with? These moments can give you clues about your passion.

Passion is important because it guides you toward your true purpose. It helps you make choices that align with who you really are. When you follow your passion, you feel more alive, more connected, and more true to yourself.

- It's not always easy to identify your passion, especially when there are so many distractions. But taking the time to explore what truly excites you can lead to a more fulfilling life. Remember, your passion is unique to you. It doesn't have to make sense to others; it just has to make sense to you.

Take a moment to reflect on what you love. Listen to your heart, and let it guide you. Your passion is there, waiting to be discovered.

Discovering Your Values

Values are the principles that guide our lives. They are what we hold dear and what makes us feel happy and fulfilled. Knowing your values helps you make decisions that are true to who you are.

Think about the moments when you felt proud or happy. What were you doing? These moments are clues to your values. For example, if you feel happy helping someone, kindness might be one of your values. If you felt proud after telling the truth, honesty might be one of your values.

Values don't have to be big or complex. They can be simple things like kindness, honesty, or family. What matters is that they are true to you.

Living according to your values makes you feel grounded and true to yourself. You make choices that align with who you are, rather than trying to fit into someone else's mould.

Take time to reflect on your actions and feelings. What makes you feel good inside? These are your values. They guide you in making decisions and help you stay true to yourself.

Knowing what you are good at helps you build a life that feels right for you.

Explore your Strengths

Look at yourself through a simple lens and see your talents, skills, and abilities. These are your strengths and these are the things you do well and enjoy doing.

Think back to a time when you felt really good about something you accomplished. Maybe it was solving a difficult problem, creating something beautiful, or helping someone in need. These moments show your strengths.

Here's a story about a man who found his strength by following his passion.

As a young man, he loved to draw. He spent hours doodling in his notebooks. But he never thought much of it. He grew up and got a job in a corporate office. His days were filled with meetings and paperwork. It was stable, but it didn't make him happy.

One day, during a particularly stressful time, he picked up his old sketchbook and started drawing again. He felt a sense of peace and joy that he hadn't felt in a long time. He realized that drawing was not just a hobby; it was a strength. It was something that made him feel alive.

He started to draw more often and even took a few art classes. His friends and family noticed his talent and encouraged him to pursue it further. So, he goes ahead and takes a leap of faith, leaving his corporate job to become a full-time artist.

At first, it was tough. He wasn't sure if he could make a living from his art. But he just kept at it, drawing every day, and little by little started making a name for himself. His hard work paid off, and today, his art is celebrated and admired by many.

This man is Leonardo Da Vinci. His journey shows how discovering and following your strengths can lead to a fulfilling and meaningful life.

To explore your strengths, start by making a list of things you enjoy and feel confident doing. Ask yourself questions like:

- What activities make me lose track of time because I enjoy them so much?
- What do people often compliment me on?
- What tasks do I find easy that others might find difficult?

You can also ask friends or family what they think your strengths are. Sometimes others see things in us that we don't notice ourselves.

Have a clear understanding on the below questions:

- *What is the core of my heart's desire?*
- *What problem do I believe requires my unique skills and talents to help resolve?*
- *What themes or topics keep recurring in my thoughts?*
- *What would bring me the greatest sense of fulfillment and joy?*

Everyone has strengths. They make you unique and are the tools you can use to build a fulfilling life. By knowing your strengths, you can focus on activities and goals that align with who you are.

Exploring your strengths is like discovering hidden treasures within yourself. It helps you discover your real potential and steers you towards a life that just feels right and fulfilling.

How do we identify our passion and values in a way that makes a difference in the world?

We all have things that make us happy. Sometimes, these passions are just for our own pleasure. For example, someone might love collecting high-end cars. This can be fun and exciting, but it mainly benefits that person. This is what we call a selfish passion.

Think about the things that make you excited. What makes you feel alive? Now, ask yourself: does this passion help anyone else, or is it mainly for my own joy? It's okay to enjoy things for yourself, but if you want to make a difference in the world, it's important to find passions that also benefit others.

How to Identify a Selfish Passion

- **Look at Your Interests**: Make a list of the things you love doing. Do you love shopping for luxury items, or do you enjoy helping others learn new skills?
- **Think About the Impact**: Consider the impact of your passion. Does it only bring joy to you, or does it help others too? Luxury cars might be fun, but teaching kids how to read can change lives.
- **Match with Values**: Compare your passion with your values. Do they match? If you're all about kindness and love helping animals, that's a great fit. But if your thing is more self-centered, it might not line up with values like kindness and compassion.
- **Use Your Strengths to Help**: Look at your strengths and see if they can be used to help others. If you're good at cooking, why not share your skills by teaching others or cooking for those in need?

The Reality of Selfish Passion

A selfish passion benefits only you. It might bring you happiness, but it does nothing for others. When you focus only on what makes you happy, you miss the chance to make a positive impact. The world doesn't change or improve from selfish passions. It stays the same, or sometimes, it even gets worse.

Collecting luxury watches might be enjoyable for you. But how does it help anyone else? It doesn't feed the hungry, educate children, or heal the sick. It's just something you do for yourself.

When people focus on selfish passions, they often feel empty after a while. They chase after things that only bring temporary joy. They miss out on the deeper satisfaction that comes from helping others and making a real difference.

Think about the world around you. What does it need? More kindness, more support, more understanding. Selfish passions do not provide these things. They only add to the noise and clutter of our lives. They don't create lasting happiness or change.

Selfish passions leave a void. They might make you happy for a moment, but they don't build a better world. The real joy and fulfillment come from passions that reach beyond ourselves and touch the lives of others.

The Answers for All

We have talked about identifying your passion, discovering your values, and exploring your strengths. We've asked so many questions on this journey. Like, how do we figure out what really excites us, you know? How do we understand what truly matters to us? How do we use our abilities to make a difference? The answer to all of these questions is simple: love.

Love is at the heart of everything. When your passion and purpose come from love, they naturally align with values that make the world better. Love drives us to look beyond ourselves and think about how we can help others. It transforms our own joy into something that benefits everyone.

When you think about your passion, consider how it can be rooted in love. Love shows you how your talents and interests can really make a positive impact, you know? It connects your strengths with actions that bring joy and meaning not just to you, but to those around you.

Your values come from love too. The things you truly care about are connected to what you love. When you act with love, your decisions show your real values. It's what makes life feel so genuine and fulfilling.

Love is the thread that ties everything together. It answers the questions about passion, values, and strengths. It guides you to use your unique abilities in ways that help others and bring happiness to your life.

By letting love guide you, you find deeper satisfaction and purpose. Love transforms your personal journey into something that touches the lives of others. It helps you understand the whole situation and see how your actions can improve the world.

> *"Not all of us can do great things. But we can do small things with great love."*
> - Mother Teresa

Destiny will unfold

As you embark on the journey of pursuing your purpose overcoming distractions and challenges, destiny begins to unfold with elegance and precision. The path ahead which was once shrouded in uncertainty will gradually illuminate revealing a tapestry of interconnected threads. With each step forward fueled by your passions, values, and experiences your destiny harmonizes with the symphony of life creating an orchestra of synchronicities and serendipities. Like a river flowing effortlessly to its destination, your life begins to align with your highest potential, and you'll find yourself exactly where you need to be, doing what you were meant to do. As you surrender to the natural flow of your purpose, you weave a narrative that is uniquely your own, a story of courage, resilience and triumph that will echo through eternity.

Conclusion

In this chapter, we've explored how purpose acts as a divine calling, leading to fulfillment. Self-awareness is essential for uncovering this purpose, as it is closely tied to your values, passions, and the experiences that shape you. As you grow through life, your understanding of purpose evolves, aligning more deeply with God's plan. Discovering your purpose requires patience and reflection, but it is this journey that brings meaning and guides your actions.

Reflective Questions

To help you further explore your purpose, consider these questions:

- *Think about the moments in your life when you felt truly alive and fulfilled. How do these experiences connect with your values and passions?*

- *How do you personally define purpose? What role does it play in your daily life?*
- *Reflect on your core values. Are they in alignment with the path you're currently pursuing?*
- *How has your idea of purpose changed over time as you've grown and faced new experiences?*
- *How does your faith influence your discovery and understanding of purpose?*

Practical Applications

Take time to reflect on your values and passions, as this can provide insight into your purpose. Identifying your strengths and talents will help you focus on areas where you can make a meaningful impact. It may help to write down long-term goals that align with your purpose, providing a clear direction for your life. Visualizing your goals, perhaps through a vision board or mind map, can bring clarity. If you're looking for additional guidance, consider tools which will make you understand your strengths.

Actionable Steps

Start by setting aside regular time each week for reflection on your purpose, ensuring you stay grounded and aligned with your goals. Research career paths or projects that resonate with your values, and find ways to integrate these into your life, whether through volunteering, side projects, or other meaningful work.

Principles

1. *Purpose is a divine calling that brings fulfillment.*
2. *Self-awareness is crucial for discovering purpose.*
3. *Values and passions intersect to reveal purpose.*
4. *Patience and reflection facilitate purpose discovery.*

Practical applications

1. *Reflect on your values and passions.*
2. *Identify your strengths and talents.*
3. *Write down your long-term goals.*
4. *Create a vision board or mind map.*

Actionable Steps

- *Schedule a weekly reflection time.*
- *Research career options aligning with your values.*
- *Volunteer or take on a side project.*

CHAPTER 2 The Search for Real Fulfillment

"Seeking fulfillment from the outside world only deepens the emptiness within."

Many people look for validation and fulfillment outside of themselves, often seeking approval through social media, following trends, or chasing after things that seem popular. It's easy to get caught up in what others think because everyone wants to feel accepted and appreciated. However, relying on others for self-worth often leads to feelings of emptiness.

When you choose to find and live your purpose, you gain the strength and clarity to overcome habits like pornography and other addictions that hold you back. Purpose fills the emptiness that often leads to these habits and gives you real fulfillment, joy, and direction. By focusing on your unique path and the difference you are meant to make, you become stronger and can break free from patterns of dependency, finding a deeper sense of freedom and self-worth. Living with purpose aligns your actions with who you are truly meant to be.

Posting pictures online and hoping for likes and comments, or buying things that aren't needed just because others have them, might provide a temporary boost, but the satisfaction doesn't last. The problem with depending on external validation is that it never truly fulfills.

When others define happiness for you, you lose control over your own well-being. Praise from others may feel good, but lack of it can leave someone feeling unworthy. This constant need for approval can be exhausting, like chasing something that can never be fully reached.

In a world where everyone is constantly connected, it's easy to forget that real fulfillment comes from within. Worth begins to be measured by how much attention is received or by how closely one matches others' standards.

This need for external validation can lead to unhealthy behaviors. Some people might push themselves too hard, not because they love what they do, but because they crave recognition. Others might change who they are, not because it brings happiness, but because they want to be admired. But even when the sought-after validation is received, it doesn't last long. Soon, there is a need for more, just to keep feeling okay.

No amount of external validation can fill the gap if there isn't a good feeling about oneself on the inside. When too much reliance is placed on others for worth, there is a risk of losing touch with who one really is. This can create a cycle where satisfaction is never fully achieved, no matter how much approval is gained.

Seeking validation from external sources can make it feel like there's always something being chased that's never truly attainable. It distracts from finding real fulfillment in things that matter—like relationships, personal growth, and inner peace.

> *One of the most harmful ways people seek external validation is through addiction to pornography.*

It's a silent crisis that's affecting millions of lives, yet we rarely talk about it openly. Pornography is everywhere—available at the click of a button—and for many, it becomes a quick escape from reality. But what starts as a simple distraction can quickly spiral into something much darker.

When people feel empty or disconnected from their lives, they often look for something to fill that void. For some, that something is porn. It offers a temporary sense of pleasure, a brief moment where they can forget about their struggles. But this escape is just that—temporary. The satisfaction doesn't last, and soon enough, they're back to feeling the same emptiness that drove them to it in the first place.

This is where the problem begins. Over time, what was once a casual habit can turn into a dependency. People start relying on porn to feel good, to feel something, anything. It becomes a way to cope with the stress, loneliness, or lack of purpose they feel in their daily lives. But instead of helping, it only makes things worse.

Porn doesn't offer real connection or fulfillment. It creates unrealistic expectations and distorts how people view themselves and others. The more someone turns to porn, the more disconnected they become from reality. This cycle can make you feel more worthless and alone.

What's happening now is a global catastrophe. Millions of people are getting caught in this trap, seeking meaning in a place where there is none. Porn addiction is not just about the act itself; it's about the loss of real, meaningful connections. It's about people trying to find fulfillment in something that ultimately leaves them feeling more empty.

This isn't just a personal issue—it's a societal one. As more people fall into this cycle, the impact on our world grows. Relationships struggle, confidence drops, and joy fades from daily life. People are living their lives in a constant state of disconnection, all while trying to fill a void that pornography can never truly satisfy.

How people seek validation from external sources like social media and pornography. There are many factors for that,

Access to Smartphones

'A person who lacks the sense of purpose, distracts himself or herself with pleasure.'

In our search for validation and fulfillment, many turn to the easy access provided by smartphones. This brings us to another important issue: how smartphones are changing the way young people experience the world.

Smartphones are everywhere. Almost everyone has one, and they have become a big part of daily life. With a smartphone, you can access information, talk to friends, and find entertainment whenever you want. But this easy access also comes with risks, especially for the younger generation.

Smartphones are more than just devices to stay in touch. They open the door to the entire internet, which includes a lot of content that isn't always healthy or appropriate. For young people, who are still figuring out who they are, this can be overwhelming.

Imagine a teenager spending hours on their phone. With just a few clicks, they can find themselves in places they weren't looking for, like explicit content or harmful trends. This constant exposure can shape the way they see themselves and the world, often in ways that aren't positive.

When a young person sees unrealistic images or ideas on their phone, it can distort their understanding of relationships, self-worth, and even their own identity. Instead of finding good role models or healthy activities, they might get caught up in things that don't help them grow or feel good about themselves.

The fact that almost every young person has a smartphone means that this problem is widespread. It's not just affecting a few people—it's impacting an entire generation. The ease with which young people can access potentially harmful content through their phones is something we can't ignore.

Easy Access to Porn Content

'In the absence of clear purpose many seek refuge in the instant gratifications of life, only to discover that the void within cannot be filled with pleasures.'

The availability of smartphones and the internet has made it incredibly easy to access pornography, creating a significant shift in how people, especially the youth, consume explicit content. This access is not limited to any one part of the world; it's a global phenomenon. However, some countries see higher levels of engagement with pornographic content than others.

The United States currently leads the world in the consumption of online pornography. Studies show that Americans make up a large percentage of global traffic to porn sites, with nearly **30%** of the global visits coming from the U.S. alone. This widespread access has significant implications for how people, particularly young people, are influenced by what they see online.

In addition to the U.S., countries like the United Kingdom, India, and Japan also rank high in terms of access to pornographic content. In the UK, around **25%** of all internet users regularly visit porn sites, while in India, the figure is slightly lower but still significant at around **20%**. Japan, known for its unique and often explicit adult content, also sees a high percentage of its population engaging with online pornography. The data shows that pornographic sites receive millions of visits every month, with the majority of users being between 18 and 34 years old.

The easy access to porn through smartphones and other devices means that young people are exposed to explicit content at a much younger age. Studies have shown that the average age of first exposure to pornography is now as young as **11 years old**. This early exposure can have long-lasting effects on how individuals perceive relationships, intimacy, and their own self-worth.

This widespread availability of porn is not just about convenience; it also has serious implications for mental health and behavior. The constant exposure to such content can also lead to unhealthy habits and dependencies, as individuals seek out more extreme content to satisfy their cravings.

The easy access to porn has created a situation where many people, especially the youth, are exposed to content that can distort their understanding of sex and relationships. This can lead to unrealistic expectations and a detachment from real-life interactions, as the constant stimulation from porn does not translate into healthy, fulfilling relationships.

Unhealthy Trends Destroying the Youth

Today's youth are facing challenges that previous generations didn't encounter, and many of these challenges come from unhealthy trends that have taken hold, especially with the rise of social media and technology.

One of the most concerning trends is the amount of time young people spend on social media. Research shows that teenagers spend hours daily scrolling through their feeds, where they see images and posts that often give an unrealistic view of life. This constant exposure is linked to increased anxiety, depression, and feelings of inadequacy. The pressure to appear perfect online can push young people to extremes, whether it's trying to look a certain way, engaging in risky behaviors, or even self-harm, all in an attempt to fit in or stand out.

Another dangerous trend is the normalization of drug and alcohol use among young people, often glamorized through social media and pop culture. This has led to more teens experimenting with substances at a younger age, with many not fully understanding the risks. The consequences can be devastating, leading to addiction and long-term health problems.

There's a disturbing trend where young people harm themselves or post negative things about themselves online, hoping to get attention or sympathy. This behavior is often a sign of deeper issues, like low self-esteem or a need for external validation, and it only adds to the mental health crisis among the youth.

These trends aren't just passing phases; they are shaping how young people see themselves and the world, often in harmful ways. The impact is real and lasting, leading to more mental health issues, dangerous behaviors, and a growing disconnection from reality.

> *This is a wake-up call that what's popular isn't always what's good, and the choices made now can have serious consequences down the road.*

The Pointlessness of External Validation

We've discussed how people often look for validation from external sources—whether through social media, addictions, or unhealthy trends. But no matter how much we chase these things, they rarely bring lasting fulfillment. The truth is, that seeking approval from others is a never-ending cycle that leaves us feeling empty.

Real meaning in life doesn't come from the approval of others or temporary pleasures. It comes from something deeper—our passion and purpose. And for that passion to truly matter, it needs to be grounded in love.

Love is what gives our lives real meaning. When your passion is driven by love, it naturally aligns with helping others and making a positive impact on the world. This kind of passion isn't about getting validation from others; it's about doing what feels right and meaningful to you.

When you follow a passion that's rooted in love—whether it's helping others, creating something beautiful, or simply living in a way that brings joy—you're not focused on what others think. Instead, you're guided by an inner sense of purpose. This is where true fulfillment comes from, and it's something that external validation can never provide.

The Dangers of Comparison

With social media, comparing ourselves to others has become almost automatic. Platforms like Instagram, Facebook, and TikTok show us only the best parts of others' lives—their successes, happiness, and picture-perfect moments. This constant exposure can make us feel like we need to measure up, which often hurts our self-esteem, mental health, and sense of purpose. When we play the comparison game, we forget our own unique journey and the qualities that make us who we are.

Social media intensifies this habit of comparison. These platforms are designed to highlight only the joyful, successful moments, giving us a distorted view of reality. As we scroll through these endless posts, it's easy to feel like everyone else has a better, happier, or more fulfilling life. This can lead to feelings of inadequacy and envy.

Social media also fuels competition. Likes, comments, and shares are seen as signs of popularity, making us feel like we need to live up to these unrealistic standards.

Influencers and public figures often show carefully curated lives, setting a bar for what success and happiness should look like. This pressure can make us feel dissatisfied with our own lives, leading us to project an ideal image online that doesn't always match who we really are.

Comparing ourselves to others can also harm our relationships. As we look at friends and acquaintances online, we might feel jealousy or resentment, which can lead us to pull away from real connections. Instead of building genuine friendships, we end up creating shallow bonds based on popularity and appearance.

Comparison also breeds discontent. It keeps us focused on what we lack, rather than appreciating our progress and strengths. The constant doubts can drown out our true purpose, making it hard to value what we have. When we compare ourselves to others, we miss the fact that everyone is on their own journey, shaped by unique experiences and challenges.

To break free from comparison, we need to look inward. This means committing to self-reflection and remembering that our worth doesn't depend on anyone else. By valuing our individuality and recognizing that our purpose is unique to us, we can find a sense of contentment that comparison can't provide. Let's remind ourselves that each of us has a purpose that deserves to be celebrated and pursued, without the need to measure up to others.

This is how we find true purpose and live a life that feels right—not because of what others think, but because it's aligned with who we truly are.

Mental Health Issues

Excessive social media use has been linked to a plethora of mental health issues, including anxiety, depression, self-esteem and body image issues, addiction, obsessive-compulsive disorder, eating disorders, and suicidal ideation. Social media platforms showcase the highlight reels of other people's lives, creating unrealistic expectations and promoting consumerism, materialism, and the cult of celebrity, leading to feelings of inadequacy, low self-esteem, and anxiety. Furthermore, social media can be a breeding ground for bullying and harassment, which can have serious negative effects on mental health, including increased symptoms of depression, anxiety, and post-traumatic stress disorder (PTSD). The constant stream of information on social media can also lead to feelings of overwhelm, stress, and burnout, as well as decreased attention span, decreased ability to focus, and decreased academic performance. Warning signs of social media-related mental health issues include excessive screen time, withdrawal from social activities, mood changes, sleep disturbances, and negative self-image. To mitigate these risks, it's essential to set boundaries, encourage physical activity, practice mindfulness, seek professional help when needed, and educate and raise awareness about the potential mental health risks associated with social media use. Additionally, parents, educators, and mental health professionals must work together to develop and implement effective strategies for promoting healthy social media use and mitigating its negative effects on mental health.

Fear of rejection

The fear of rejection and difficulty with self-acceptance are two interconnected issues that can arise when youth rely on external validation rather than developing a sense of self-worth. The fear of rejection can lead to social anxiety, people-pleasing, difficulty setting boundaries, and hypersensitivity to criticism, causing youth to become overly concerned with what others think of them. Meanwhile, difficulty with self-acceptance can lead to self-doubt, negative self-talk, constant comparison to others, difficulty regulating emotions, and struggles with identity formation, ultimately hindering youth from developing a positive and authentic sense of self.

Start Now

Take the first step towards unlocking your true potential by embracing your passions and pursuing your purpose. Start by exploring your interests, values, and strengths, and identify what truly sets your soul on fire. Don't be afraid to take risks, learn from failures, and seek guidance from others. As you embark on this journey, you'll find that you're no longer held captive by the chains of addiction, whether it's to porn, social media, or the constant need for external validation. You'll break free from the fear of rejection and the constant seeking of approval from others. You'll also find that mental health issues such as anxiety, depression, and low self-esteem will begin to fade away. Remember, your God given purpose is unique to you, and it's the key to living a life that's authentic, fulfilling, and meaningful. So, start now, and watch your life transform into a journey of purpose, passion, and happiness.

Conclusion

In this chapter, we discussed how relying on external sources like social media, unhealthy habits, or addictions for approval or fulfillment can leave us feeling empty. Depending on outside validation takes us further from real contentment. True fulfillment comes from within, by understanding our passions and values and building meaningful relationships. Focusing on self-awareness and what genuinely matters helps us break free from the endless need for external approval.

Reflective Questions

Take a moment to reflect on these questions as you continue your journey toward true fulfillment:

- *How has your relationship with social media or smartphones affected your self-worth and your relationships with others?*
- *What are the deeper emotions or needs behind any habits or addictions you're struggling with? Are you trying to fill a gap with these behaviors?*
- *What new, healthier habits can you start that align with your personal growth and purpose?*
- *In difficult moments, how do you practice kindness and self-compassion toward yourself?*
- *Who can you turn to for support and accountability during this process of change?*

Practical Applications

Start by taking a look at how your current habits might be impacting your life. Set limits on how much time you spend on your phone, especially on activities that don't add value to your life. Take time to reflect on your passions and what really matters to you. Writing down your goals and thinking about how they align with your values can help give you direction. Mindfulness, journaling, or spending time on hobbies can help ground you in what's meaningful. Don't be afraid to reach out to friends, family, or support groups if you need help along the way.

Actionable Steps

Set some time each day to reflect on your habits and consider deleting or limiting your use of social media. Create "phone-free" hours during the day to help you stay more present. Explore new hobbies or activities that align with your passions. Volunteering or taking up a creative project can help you reconnect with yourself. If it's challenging to maintain boundaries, consider using tools like website blockers to create space for healthier habits. Remember to be patient with yourself as you make these changes, and reach out for support when needed.

Principles

1. *Addiction masks underlying purpose deficits.*
2. *True validation comes from within and meaningful relationships.*
3. *Digital detox is essential for clarity.*
4. *Healthy habits replace addictive behaviors.*

Questions

1. *How have digital habits impacted your relationships and self-perception?*
2. *What underlying needs drive your addiction to porn or smartphones?*
3. *What alternative habits can you adopt to cultivate self-awareness and purpose?*
4. *How do you practice self-compassion in times of struggle?*
5. *Who can you turn to for accountability and support?*

Actionable Steps

1. *Set boundaries on screen time.*
2. *Replace phone habits with reading or journaling and start working on your passion.*
3. *Join a support group or accountability partner.*
4. *Practice mindfulness and self-compassion.*

CHAPTER 3 Breaking Down Divides

"What counts in life is not the mere fact that we have lived. It is what difference we have made to the lives of others that will determine the significance of the life we lead."

- Nelson Mandela

We all have a purpose, and that purpose is not determined by caste, race, or social status. It's something that comes from within and can be discovered by anyone, regardless of where they were born. Breaking down divides is like sitting at a large table where everyone has different meals in front of them. At first, people are focused on their own plates, not really looking at what anyone else is eating. Some plates have more food, some less, and some dishes look completely unfamiliar. Everyone is quiet, keeping to themselves.

But then, someone asks, "What's that on your plate?" Slowly, conversations start. People begin sharing what they have, explaining their food, and offering others a taste. Before long, the table that felt disconnected became lively, with everyone passing plates and trying different things.

The table hasn't changed—everyone still has their own meal—but now, instead of feeling separate, they are connected through sharing. This is how divides break down. It doesn't happen by erasing what's different; it happens when people take the time to share and understand. Everyone at the table brings something valuable, and the experience becomes richer when they come together.

It's a simple act of reaching out and asking, but it changes everything. The divides that once seemed so strong start to disappear when people realize that, deep down, they all have something to share.

> *The barriers between people shouldn't define a person's worth or purpose. A person's worth should be defined by their inherent qualities, talents and potential. Let's look at how these divides shape our world and why they no longer hold the weight they once did.*

Racial Divides

Racial divides have existed for a long time, affecting how people are treated based on their race or skin color. These divides can be traced back to events in history like the invasions, colonialism, slavery, and segregation, which created unfair systems where some groups were seen as better than others.

Invasions

Invasions have led to the displacement and devastation of countless communities throughout history. The Mongol invasions of the 13th century, for example, resulted in widespread destruction and loss of life. The Spanish conquest of the Aztec and Inca empires in the 16th century led to the deaths of millions of indigenous people. The Scramble for Africa in the late 19th century saw European powers invade and colonize nearly the entire continent. Invasions have often been driven by a desire for resources, territory, and power, leaving deep scars on the invaded populations.

Colonialism

Colonialism was when some European countries took control of other nations and regions. This began in the 1400s and continued for centuries. The colonizers saw the people in these lands as less important and often forced them to work under harsh conditions. They brought their own culture, language, and religion, leaving the local people with little choice. Over time, this created a belief that some people were more important than others, which divided societies based on race.

Slavery

Another major cause of racial divides was the transatlantic slave trade. From the 1500s to the 1800s, millions of people were captured and sold as slaves. These people were treated like property, denied basic human rights, and forced into hard labor. People were mistreated based on their color and color was used to justify this treatment.

Even after slavery ended, the belief in racial superiority continued. Former slaves and their families struggled for many years to gain equality. There are places were racial divides are still visible in the differences in wealth, education, and opportunities between various communities.

Segregation

Segregation, or the separation of racial groups, made racial divides even worse. In the United States, laws called "Jim Crow" laws kept Black and white people apart in schools, buses, and public spaces for many years. These laws made sure that Black people had fewer rights and worse conditions.

In South Africa, apartheid was a system that separated people based on race. It started in 1948 and lasted until 1994. Under apartheid, the white minority had most of the power, while the Black majority lived in poor conditions and had very few rights. Although both segregation have ended, the damage they caused still affects people today.

The Modern Reality of Racism

Even today, racism continues to affect many communities around the world, especially those who have been historically marginalized. While laws and policies have changed to promote equality, the reality is that racism still exists in everyday life. It shows up in subtle, and sometimes not-so-subtle, ways. People from minority groups often face discrimination, which limits their access to opportunities and resources. This discrimination takes a heavy toll on both individuals and entire communities.

One of the biggest challenges with racism today is that it's often built into the systems that are supposed to serve everyone equally. This is called "systemic racism." It means that, even though there might not be any openly racist laws, the rules and practices of certain institutions, like schools, workplaces, or the justice system—still treat people differently based on their race.

For example, in many countries, Black, Indigenous, and other people of color are less likely to receive the same quality of education as white students. Schools in areas with predominantly minority populations often have fewer resources, outdated textbooks, and underpaid teachers. This gap in education means that many children from marginalized communities don't have the same chances to succeed as others. This disadvantage follows them throughout their lives, limiting their job opportunities and earning potential.

In the workplace, systemic racism shows up through wage gaps, hiring discrimination, and lack of representation. Many people of color find themselves paid less than their white counterparts, even when they have the same qualifications. Some struggle to even get their foot in the door, as racial biases often play a role in who gets hired and who gets promoted. These barriers make it harder for individuals from marginalized groups to break the cycle of poverty and climb the social ladder.

Beyond the systems, there are social biases that also create racial divides. These biases are often rooted in stereotypes and misconceptions about certain races. People from marginalized groups might be unfairly judged because of the color of their skin, their culture, or where they come from.

These social biases affect how people are treated in everyday life. Someone might face discrimination when applying for housing, experience biased policing, or be treated unfairly in social settings. These experiences can be exhausting and isolating, leading to feelings of frustration and helplessness.

For example, in many countries, Black men are more likely to be stopped by the police, regardless of whether they have done anything wrong. These biases create a sense of fear and mistrust between communities and the institutions that are supposed to protect them.

George, a Black man, was stopped by police in Minneapolis, and during the arrest, a white police officer pressed his knee on George's neck for over nine minutes. Despite George repeatedly saying he couldn't breathe, the officer didn't stop. This was all captured on video, and the footage was shared worldwide.

This incident led to protests in many countries, with people speaking out against racism and police violence. It became clear that the problem wasn't just about one incident, but about how people of color, especially Black individuals, are often treated unfairly by the police. George Floyd's death became a symbol of how racial inequality still exists in society today, reminding everyone that change is still needed.

The constant exposure to racism, whether through systemic inequalities or social biases, takes a toll on individuals and communities. People who experience racism often deal with higher levels of stress, anxiety, and depression. It's not just about being treated unfairly—it's about living in a world where you are constantly reminded that you are seen as "less than."

Communities that face racism are often stuck in cycles of poverty and disadvantage. Lack of access to quality education, healthcare, and job opportunities means that future generations are also affected. This creates a cycle that is hard to break. Racism doesn't just harm individuals; it holds back entire communities from thriving.

Caste Divides

Caste systems exist in different forms around the world, but they all share a common idea: people are divided into groups based on birth, and these groups determine their place in society. One of the most well-known examples is in India, where the caste system has existed for thousands of years. In this system, people were separated into different categories based on their jobs, such as priests, warriors, traders, and laborers. Over time, these categories became strict, and people were born into their caste with no way to change it.

But caste systems are not limited to India. Similar divisions have existed in other parts of the world too. In some places, people were ranked by their family background or by their role in society. These were often used to control groups of people, making sure certain groups had more power and privileges while others were kept at the bottom.

The problem with the caste system is that it treats people unfairly. It gives some groups more value than others, simply because of the family they were born into. This means that many people, no matter how talented or hardworking they are, are limited by the caste they belong to. This creates inequality and stops people from being treated equally.

Even though some places have tried to move away from caste systems, the effects of these divides still exist today. Many people still face discrimination because of their caste, and these old beliefs continue to shape how societies function. It's important to understand that caste-based divides have always been about keeping certain groups in power while holding others back.

A well-known example of how caste affects society today comes from the story of **Dr. B.R. Ambedkar**, a man born into the Dalit caste, which was considered "untouchable." Ambedkar faced discrimination throughout his life, especially in school. As a child, he was not allowed to sit with other students and often had to learn by standing at the back of the classroom. Despite these challenges, Ambedkar went on to become one of the most educated men of his time, earning multiple degrees from prestigious institutions like Columbia University and the London School of Economics.

Ambedkar's success didn't come easily. His caste background meant he had to fight harder than others for opportunities. Even after his education, he continued to face prejudice in his professional life. But instead of giving up, he used his experiences to fight against the caste system. Ambedkar played a key role in drafting the Indian Constitution and dedicated his life to fighting for the rights of Dalits and other marginalized groups.

Many people today, like Ambedkar in his time, still face similar barriers when trying to access education or career opportunities. Caste continues to influence who gets ahead and who is left behind. Even in modern times, people born into lower castes often struggle to break free from the limitations imposed on them by birth.

> *Access to quality education, healthcare, and employment is still unequal for many people in lower castes.*

Hierarchy is Invalid

For centuries, the idea of a caste-based hierarchy has suggested that some people are born to lead and others are meant to follow, simply because of the family they were born into. This belief has kept many people in lower positions, without considering their potential or individual strengths. But this way of thinking is flawed. It assumes that a person's worth is decided at birth, and that's not true.

Every person, no matter their caste or background, has the potential to lead, create, and contribute to society in meaningful ways. History has shown time and again that people from all walks of life have made significant changes in the world. The idea that some are "better" than others because of their birth is outdated. What really matters is a person's abilities, passion, and drive to make a difference.

The Universal Truth of Equality

The truth is simple: every human being is equal. We are all born with the ability to find our purpose and contribute to the world in our own way. No one is superior or inferior because of their caste or race. What defines a person is their character, their actions, and how they use their strengths to make a positive impact.

The idea of caste-based hierarchy tries to put limits on people, but these limits aren't real. They are constructed by society and can be broken.

> *"For a successful revolution, it is not enough that there is discontent. What is required is a profound and thorough conviction of the justice, necessity, and importance of political and social rights."*
>
> *— Bhim Rao Ambedkar*

Purpose is Not Defined by Caste or Race

Your purpose is something you discover for yourself. It isn't determined by where you're born, the family you come from, or the color of your skin. Caste, race, or any other label society places on people doesn't have the power to define who you are or what you're meant to do in life.

These things might shape your environment, but they do not define your potential or your path.

For centuries, societies have tried to organize people into groups based on these external factors. Caste systems and racial hierarchies were built on the idea that some people were more important than others simply because of birth. But the truth is, such things dictate no person's purpose in life. Purpose comes from within—it's about understanding your values, your passions, and your strengths.

Each person has a unique role to play, and it's up to them to discover what that is. It might take time to find it, but it's there, waiting to be uncovered. No matter what society says, no one can take that away from you.

Living your Purpose in life

Living a life with purpose means going beyond the limits that caste, race, or skin color might try to place on you. It's about breaking free from the ideas that tell you what you can and cannot do based on your background. Your purpose is for you to find. It's not something society gives you; it's something you find by exploring what really matters to you.

A purposeful life is built on understanding your values—what's important to you. It's also about recognizing your God given passions, the things that excite you and make you feel alive. And it's about knowing your strengths, those talents, and skills that come naturally to you and allow you to make a difference.

When you live in alignment with these things, you live fully. You're not limited by the expectations of others or by the restrictions society places on you. Instead, you're driven by what makes you feel whole and connected to the world around you.

There's great freedom in knowing that your purpose is your own. It doesn't have to fit into anyone else's idea of what's right or wrong. It doesn't matter what caste or race you belong to—your purpose is bigger than any label. By discovering and living your purpose, you break free from the old structures that try to keep people in certain roles. You live for something bigger, something true to who you really are.

Each person's journey is different. Some might find their purpose early, while others might take longer. But the important thing is to keep exploring, keep learning about yourself, and stay open to where your heart leads you.

> *No matter where you come from, the world needs your unique contributions, and your purpose will always be a part of making that difference.*

Conclusion

The truth is that everyone has a purpose, and it isn't defined by where they come from or the color of their skin. Our purpose comes from within, from our values, passions, and strengths. When we live with purpose, we can start to break down these divisions, bringing people together through understanding and respect.

Reflective Questions

Here are some questions to think about as you reflect on what we've discussed:

- *Have racial or caste barriers affected you or the people around you? How do these divides show up in your life or community?*

- *How do your beliefs or faith challenge these divides and encourage equality?*
- *Can you think of a time when you connected with someone from a different background? What did you learn from that experience?*
- *What small steps can you take in your daily life to promote equality and understanding?*
- *How can focusing on your purpose help you and others break down these social barriers?*

Practical Applications

- Start by having open, honest conversations with people from different backgrounds. Sharing your experiences and listening to others can help break down walls and stereotypes.
- Read books or attend events that focus on diversity and inclusion. Learning from others can open your eyes to the challenges they face and help you become part of the solution.
- Get involved in your community. Volunteering with organizations that support equality can make a real difference in promoting understanding and unity.

*Everyone's Got a Purpose - Beyond Racial Divisions and Caste Hierarchies**

Principles

1. *Purpose transcends artificial racial and caste barriers.*
2. *Racial and caste divisions are human-made constructs, not divine design.*
3. *Every individual has inherent value and purpose.*
4. *Purpose is not limited by societal expectations or hierarchies.*
5. *Caste and racial divisions are meaningless.*
6. *Purposeful living dismantles social constructs.*
7. *Every individual has unique gifts and contributions, regardless of background.*

Questions

1. *How have racial or caste divisions impacted your life or community?*
2. *What principles challenge these social constructs?*
3. *Share experiences of meaningful connections across racial or caste lines.*
4. *How can we promote unity and equality in our daily lives?*
5. *What role does purpose play in breaking down social barriers?*

Actionable Steps

1. *Engage in cross-cultural conversations.*
2. *Read books on diversity and inclusion.*
3. *Attend community events or workshops.*
4. *Volunteer with organizations promoting social justice.*
5. *Reflect on personal biases and privilege.*

CHAPTER

4 Growing Beyond Limits

'The war against terrorism must also be a war on purposelessness and on addressing the root causes of disaffection and despair that can drive individuals to extremist's ideologies.'

We live in a world filled with invisible walls, barriers that stop people from understanding each other. These walls aren't always built with bricks, but with fear, mistrust, and beliefs that push people apart. You can see it in the news, hear it in conversations, and feel it when communities grow distant. When these barriers go up, it becomes harder for people to connect, and to see things from another perspective.

Breaking these barriers is not just about tearing down walls of misunderstanding, but about recognizing how deeply they affect everyone. They don't only harm the people directly involved, but they spread fear, anger, and division throughout society. The world becomes smaller and more isolated, and we all feel the weight of these walls in some way.

When people lack purpose, they can feel empty and become more open to negative influences, including extreme ideas. Without a sense of direction or belief in their own worth, some may look for meaning in harmful causes, thinking it will make them feel fulfilled. But when people discover their true, God-given purpose, they grow stronger against these influences by focusing on positive values. Purpose gives them a clear path, helping them contribute to society in helpful ways instead of turning to violence or extreme beliefs. Living with purpose not only changes personal lives but also makes communities stronger and safer.

The Roots of Fear: Terrorism

Terrorism often starts with fear. It's born from a place where people feel threatened—whether it's their beliefs, way of life, or safety. When fear grows, it turns into anger and then into violence. People who are scared of losing what they know can sometimes feel like the only option is to strike first. That's when terrorism takes root.

Fear leads to misunderstanding, and misunderstanding creates divides. When one group fears another, they stop talking, they stop trying to understand. This is how terrorism finds its power. It feeds on these divides, and as the gap grows between people, it becomes harder to close.

Wars only add to this. We see how terrorism and war go hand in hand, each one making the other worse. Communities are torn apart, leaving scars that don't heal easily. People who have lost their homes, loved ones, or sense of safety are left with a deep wound. They carry that hurt, and it spreads, sometimes even to the next generation.

The scars left by terrorism are not just physical. They live in people's minds, affecting how they see the world, how they trust others, and how they live their lives. Fear, when it takes hold, doesn't go away easily. It changes everything, for individuals and for entire societies.

It doesn't just hurt the people directly affected; it impacts everyone, no matter where they live. When an attack happens, fear spreads, and that fear changes how people feel about their own safety. We see it on the news, and suddenly, places that once felt safe no longer do. It makes people more cautious, and more worried, and it can be hard to go about life without thinking about the possibility of danger.

For those who go through it firsthand, the pain is much deeper. They carry the emotional weight of what happened, and it can be hard to feel safe again. But even those watching from a distance are affected. It's natural to wonder, "Could this happen where I am?" This kind of thinking becomes part of everyday life, making people more alert and on edge.

On a larger scale, terrorism changes how countries work together. Governments make new rules, tighten security, and focus on protecting their citizens. While these changes are meant to keep people safe, they can also change how we live, travel, and communicate. We see more checks, and more restrictions, and often feel like the world is becoming less open.

The emotional impact is heavy. It's not just fear of an attack, but the worry about what the future holds. People feel unsure about their safety, their families, and the world around them. These feelings don't just go away, they affect how people live their daily lives.

> *Terrorism doesn't stop at one event. It's a cycle of fear that can be hard to break, and it leaves a lasting mark on the world.*

Beyond the Boundaries: Extremism

Extremism doesn't always show up as violence. Sometimes, it sneaks into our daily lives through extreme beliefs that seem harmless at first but slowly push people toward harmful actions. These radical ideas can divide people and make them see the world in black and white, creating an "us vs. them" mentality.

These extreme ideologies feed into terrorism. They create an environment where people feel justified in using violence to defend their beliefs. The more divided society becomes, the easier it is for extremism to grow. It fuels hatred and mistrust, making people feel that anyone who doesn't agree with them is the enemy.

Extremism affects communities by driving people apart. It stops conversations, it stops understanding, and it makes fear the main way people relate to each other. When people are divided, it becomes easier for violence to seem like a solution. This is the real danger of extremism—it doesn't just live in the shadows; it grows in plain sight, in everyday life, slowly pushing people toward dangerous actions.

When individuals or entire communities become locked into extreme beliefs, their world becomes small. They stop listening to different ideas, and this blocks personal growth. They stay within the same narrow view of life, convinced that their way is the only way. This limited thinking creates a wall, stopping any kind of progress, both for the individual and the society around them.

When people are stuck in such a mindset, they can't see the world for what it really is—a place filled with different perspectives, ideas, and experiences. Instead, they only see what fits their beliefs. This limits how much they can grow as people. They stop learning, stop questioning, and stop evolving.

Extremism isolates, and in that isolation, both individuals and societies become stuck.

The Power of Learning: Skill-Based Training

One of the most effective ways to do this is through skill-based training. Learning practical skills can make a real difference in someone's life. It gives people the tools they need to take control of their own future.

Skill-based training isn't just about learning for the sake of it. It's about gaining abilities that can be used in real life—things that can help someone find a job, start a business, or simply feel more confident in their abilities. Whether it's learning a trade, mastering technology, or developing creative skills, practical knowledge builds a foundation for personal growth.

This kind of training goes beyond just professional benefits. It builds self-reliance and confidence. When people learn a new skill, they see their own potential, and that makes a huge difference in how they approach life. They're able to contribute not just to their own lives but also to their communities, helping to rebuild and strengthen the bonds that have been damaged.

The real strength of learning lies in how it changes a person's view of themselves. It's not just about the technical skills, they are important, but it's about realizing that growth is possible. People start to see opportunities where they once saw limitations. It opens up doors that were once closed, allowing them to create a meaningful life filled with purpose.

In his early life, a young man dropped out of college after just one semester. He didn't have a clear direction but chose to stay close to campus, taking courses that interested him, like calligraphy. He slept on friends' floors and searched for meaning in his life. After a journey to India he returned home with a focus on simplicity and design. Despite not following the usual path, he started working on a project that would later grow into something much bigger.

This young man faced rejection too. He was fired from the very company he helped create. But instead of letting that stop him, he used it as a turning point. He kept learning, started a new company, and eventually made a return to his first venture. The skills he had picked up, the lessons learned from every failure, and his focus on building something meaningful allowed him to change the world in ways few could imagine.

This man is Steve Jobs, the co-founder of Apple, who transformed technology with his vision

Creating Your Path: Passion-Based Entrepreneurship

Turning what you love into a career is one of the most fulfilling paths you can take. When your work is something you're passionate about, it doesn't feel like a burden. It becomes part of who you are. Passion-based entrepreneurship is about doing what makes you feel alive and building something meaningful from it.

Many people are held back by limiting beliefs. They think they can't turn their passions into a career, or they worry about failing. But entrepreneurship offers a way to break free from those thoughts. It allows you to create your own path, to build something that reflects who you are and what you care about. When you follow your passion, you work with a sense of purpose, and that gives you the energy to keep going, even when challenges arise.

Entrepreneurship isn't just about personal success; it can also have a positive impact on the community. When you create a business around something you love, you're providing a service or product—you're also inspiring others. You show them that it's possible to follow their dreams, to turn passion into something real. This creates a ripple effect, encouraging others to think bigger and pursue their own ideas.

Building something you're passionate about can lead to growth, both for yourself and for those around you. It creates resilience because when you care deeply about what you're doing, you're more likely to stick with it through tough times. And over time, this can lead to a better future for yourself, your community, and even beyond.

Following your passion isn't just a dream—it's a path to growth, fulfillment, and positive change.

Conclusion

When individuals don't have meaning in their lives, they may feel lost or disconnected, making them more likely to turn to harmful beliefs. To prevent this, we need to focus on fixing the problems at the root, through education, creating equality, and engaging with our communities. Helping young people find purpose gives them hope and keeps them away from negative influences. When people feel connected and valued, the chances of them becoming isolated or radicalized go down. Living with a clear purpose brings peace to both individuals and society as a whole.

Reflective Questions

Take a moment to think about these questions:

- *What are the main reasons that people in your community might become radicalized? How can these issues be solved?*
- *How can education and mentorship guide young people toward a meaningful and positive life?*
- *What kind of programs can help reduce the social and economic problems that lead to extremism?*
- *How can we encourage more people to get involved in their communities and stay connected?*
- *How does having a clear purpose help promote peace, both for individuals and society?*

Practical Applications

Start by learning more about the causes of extremism. Support groups and organizations that work against terrorism and promote peace. Being involved in your community through volunteering can help build a sense of belonging. In your everyday life, practice empathy by listening and understanding others' experiences. Fostering personal growth and learning will help you and others avoid falling into harmful paths.

Actionable Steps

Volunteer with organizations that focus on preventing extremism or supporting affected communities. Attend community discussions on terrorism and extremism to understand how you and others can help. Get involved by writing to your local representatives and advocating for policies that support education, equality, and community engagement.

Principles

1. *Purposelessness fuels extremism.*
2. *Addressing root causes prevents radicalization.*
3. *Empowering youth fosters purpose.*
4. *Education addresses socioeconomic inequalities.*
5. *Community engagement counters isolation.*

Questions

1. *What factors contribute to radicalization, and how can communities prevent it?*
2. *How can education and mentorship programs promote purpose among youth?*
3. *What initiatives can address economic and social inequalities driving extremism?*
4. *How can community outreach programs foster engagement?*
5. *What role does purpose play in promoting peace?*

Actionable Steps

- *Focus on identifying your passion and purpose.*
- *Work towards your passion and get equipped in various skills relevant to your passion*
- *Plan on starting your own start-up based on your passion.*

CHAPTER 5 The Rise of False Feminism and Toxic Masculinity

'Complementary not competing relationships between men and women unlock the full potential of humanity'

Over time, feminism has changed in many ways. In its early days, the movement focused on fighting for equality, making sure that women had the same rights and opportunities as men. The goal was clear: women should have access to education, the right to vote, and equal treatment in society and the workplace. Feminism was about creating a level playing field where women could stand on equal ground with men.

But today, we sometimes see a shift from those core values. What some call "false feminism" has emerged, where the focus seems to have moved away from equality and purpose. Instead, it leans heavily on individual achievements and the idea that success is defined by working alone or against men. This version of feminism often pushes women to feel that they must do it all—be successful in every area of life, sometimes even at the cost of rejecting their natural strengths and roles.

In this view, being a woman is tied more to proving a point than accepting the value of who they are. It can create a culture where women feel pressured to fit into a narrow definition of success, one that overlooks the importance of balance, family, and community. The danger here is that it divides rather than unites, making empowerment seem like a battle to win instead of a journey of growth and contribution.

False feminism often measures progress by how much a woman can achieve on her own, ignoring the broader impact on society. This leads to a focus on individualism, where the value is placed more on personal milestones than on how those achievements benefit the community or strengthen relationships. In this way, false feminism can push women into roles that may not align with their natural strengths, leading to frustration and burnout.

Toxic masculinity refers to an unhealthy societal expectation that promote aggressive and dominant behavior in men, perpetuating the idea that men must be tough, emotionless, and in control. This toxic ideology is damaging to men's mental health, leading to increased stress, anxiety, and depression. It also contributes to violence against women and other marginalized groups. Toxic masculinity is often linked to patriarchal ideologies and power structures, restricting men's emotional expression and leading to feelings of isolation and disconnection. It manifests in behaviors like aggression, bullying, and sexual harassment, and is perpetuated through media representation, cultural norms, and socialization. Challenging toxic masculinity requires a shift in societal expectations and cultural norms. By promoting purpose driven healthy masculinity, we can create a more inclusive and equitable society for all.

Equal But Different

Men and women are equal in their value as human beings, but they have different strengths and roles in life. This doesn't mean one is better than the other—just that they bring different things to the table. By recognizing and appreciating these differences, we allow both to thrive without feeling like they need to compete.

Women often have a natural ability to nurture and connect emotionally with others, while men might focus on strength or protection. These qualities aren't about limitations—they're about how both men and women can contribute in their own ways. When we stop trying to make men and women fit the same mold, we can see that each has something important to offer.

True empowerment doesn't come from proving that one gender can do everything the other can. It comes from understanding and using the unique strengths of each, working together rather than against each other. When we celebrate these differences, it allows both men and women to grow and contribute to the world in meaningful ways.

Complementary, Not Competing

There's a growing issue where women, in trying to prove their capability, push themselves into direct competition with men. This attitude turns everyday life into a battlefield, where the focus shifts from collaboration to dominance. When women constantly feel the need to prove they can outdo men, it leads to unnecessary tension and creates a divide between the genders.

This competing nature, instead of highlighting women's natural strengths, forces them into a space where they measure success by how well they can mimic or outperform men. In doing so, the unique qualities that women bring to the table are often lost. It's not about working alongside men but about showing they can "win." This approach only weakens the potential for real empowerment because it becomes less about collaboration and more about beating the other side.

When women push themselves into competition rather than recognizing how their strengths fit with men's, the situation becomes more about pride than progress.

> *This mindset creates friction, where empowerment is seen as proving a point rather than building something meaningful together.*

Nurturers

Women have always played the role of nurturers and caregivers. This isn't just a function—it's a natural strength that helps families and communities grow and stay strong. But in recent times, many women have begun to see these roles in a negative light, as if caring for others somehow limits them or holds them back. There's a shift where some women reject these roles, trying to prove they can do more as if nurturing isn't valuable enough.

This trend ignores how important caregiving truly is. When women step away from these roles, it leaves a gap. Families lose emotional support, and communities feel less connected. Nurturing is what keeps bonds strong, whether between parents and children or within a wider community. It's a role that shapes the future and keeps society stable.

By pushing away from these natural abilities, women are often left feeling disconnected from what they're truly capable of. This isn't about limiting women to one role but acknowledging that caregiving isn't a weakness. It's a strength, and when it's neglected, everyone feels the loss.

The question is, what happens when nurturing is no longer valued?

In a country like India, as more women pursue independence and careers, there's been a shift away from traditional roles like caregiving. Many women now see these roles as less important, focusing more on individual success and proving their ability to compete in the workforce. This change might seem like progress, but it has also created problems.

Women who once played a central role in nurturing families are now often torn between work and home. The nurturing and caregiving that women naturally provided, whether for children or elderly family members, has started to disappear. As women focus on their careers, there's less time for the emotional support and care that families rely on. This shift is especially noticeable in cities, where the pressure to succeed professionally is higher.

In many parts of India, 84% of caregiving is still done by women. But now, balancing work with these duties has become harder. The focus on being independent and achieving success has made caregiving feel like a burden for some, rather than a valuable role. This is causing a gap in families, where the emotional bond and stability that caregiving provides are fading.

As women step away from their traditional nurturing roles, the family structure in many

> *cases weakens. The balance between personal success and caregiving is becoming harder to maintain, and this is changing how families function.*

Many women today hold significant influence in their families, communities, and society, but not all are using this influence in ways that lead to positive outcomes. Instead of guiding their families with understanding and support, some use their position to exert control or push personal agendas, which can strain relationships.

In communities, instead of working together for collective growth, there are instances where influence is used to create division or fuel competition. This misuse of influence can lead to friction and undermine the sense of unity that it's needed for a community to thrive.

While many women have the power to challenge norms and drive change, some focus on personal achievements without considering the larger impact on others. This kind of influence doesn't bring about the positive change that could benefit everyone. Instead, it becomes more about individual success, leaving behind the opportunity to uplift those around them.

In the name of empowerment and feminism, many women today reject the idea of submission, seeing it as a sign of weakness or inferiority. But submission in certain roles is not about being less important or valuable. It's about recognizing the natural order and authority in specific spaces. The push for women to be equal to men has, in some cases, shifted from equality to a desire for superiority. Instead of understanding their unique space in the world, many women now compete with men, striving to prove they can do everything men can.

This approach misunderstands the core idea of empowerment. Women have their own strengths and roles that are just as important as men's, but they are different. The attempt to blur the lines between men and women, to the point where some believe that women can or should take on traditionally male roles, goes against cultural norms that have existed for centuries. By fighting for superiority, women lose sight of the balance that naturally exists between men and women.

The notion that a woman should compete with a man in every aspect of life leads to confusion and unnecessary conflict. No matter how much society pushes this narrative, a woman can never be a man. The roles, strengths, and purposes are different, and that difference is not something to be fought against, but something to be understood. When women reject submission, they are often rejecting the space that allows them to flourish in their own way, trying instead to take on roles that do not align with their nature.

In doing so, they not only disrupt cultural norms but also undermine their own empowerment. True strength comes from understanding one's role and purpose, not from trying to take over someone else's.

Empowerment through purpose

Women's true liberation comes when they understand their unique strengths and how they can contribute to the betterment of their family, community, and society. It's not about trying to take on roles that don't naturally fit them but about recognizing what they are good at and using those talents to create a positive impact. When women work in ways that align with their purpose, they add value to their personal lives and to the world around them.

Women can create stability within families by being strong emotional anchors. Their natural nurturing and supportive roles allow them to strengthen relationships, foster growth, and provide balance in times of hardship. In a broader sense, when women focus on their purpose, they contribute to society by driving meaningful change, through leadership, teaching, caregiving, or creative roles.

Empowerment doesn't come from trying to do everything or proving oneself in areas that don't fit. Instead, it comes from understanding what you are good at and using that to improve the world around you. Women who focus on their talents and passions can help create stronger families and communities. They offer guidance, encouragement, and strength to those they influence, and that spreads beyond their immediate to circle.

By using their unique skills, women have the power to inspire others, create positive changes, and build a society that values both individual contribution and collective well-being.

False feminism focuses too much on personal success without considering the larger picture. When women step away from their natural roles to compete with men, it can lead to stress, frustration, and disconnection from what truly matters. The pressure to constantly achieve can cause them to lose sight of the importance of their role in the family and society.

This leads to societal imbalance, as the core values that keep communities strong—support, nurturing, and connection—are weakened. The focus on individual gain creates a sense of isolation and burnout, rather than the fulfillment that comes from living according to one's strengths.

Women, when driven by false feminism, may miss the opportunity to contribute in ways that would benefit the people and the world around them.

A God-given purpose can help resolve toxic masculinity by redefining masculinity, encouraging emotional expression and vulnerability, and promoting accountability and responsibility. It fosters compassion, empathy, and healthy relationships, inspiring personal growth and transformation. By breaking free from societal pressures and expectations, men can find a more authentic sense of purpose and identity, restoring a healthy, positive, and life-giving expression of masculinity.

Conclusion

How gender roles are understood in a way that values both men and women equally? These roles aren't about one being above the other, but about working together. Complementary relationships are about mutual support, where both people contribute their strengths. True feminism values partnership, where both men and women help each other grow. Equality is part of God's design, showing us that everyone has worth. By focusing on collaboration, we can fulfill a shared purpose, working together to honor each other and God's plan.

Reflective Questions

Here are some questions to think about as you reflect on gender roles and equality:

- *How have gender expectations from society shaped your life and the way you see your relationships?*
- *What does a complementary partnership mean to you? How can you apply this idea in your relationships?*
- *Can you think of a time when mutual support between men and women led to something positive?*
- *How do you see equality in your relationships, whether with friends, family, or coworkers?*
- *How do you understand the roles of men and women?*

Practical Applications

It's important to take time to learn more about teachings on gender roles. Open discussions about feminism and faith can help bridge understanding, creating space for men and women to support each other. Getting involved with organizations that empower women is another way to help foster equality. Take time to reflect on any personal biases, and work towards building strong, respectful relationships where both people feel valued.

Actionable Steps

You can plan to attend a conference on how faith and feminism can work together for equality.

The next suggestion would be to volunteer with an organization that focuses on women's empowerment, supporting their growth in both personal and professional spaces. For men the call to action would be to organize a conference on how to tackle and bring awareness on toxic masculinity.

Principles

1. *Gender roles are redefined in the transformative concept.*
2. *Complementary not competing relationships empower both sexes.*
3. *True feminism values mutual support.*
4. *Equality honors God's design.*
5. *Collaboration promotes shared purpose.*

Questions

1. *How have societal gender expectations impacted your life and relationships?*
2. *What does complementary partnership mean to you, and how can it be applied?*
3. *Share experiences of mutual support and empowerment.*
4. *How does equality manifest in your relationships?*

Actionable Steps

- *Attend/Organize a conference on faith and feminism/ Toxic masculinity.*
- *Volunteer with a women's empowerment organization/ Male awareness groups.*
- *Engage in discussions on feminism, masculinity and faith.*
- *Support organizations empowering women and those which bring awareness on toxic masculinity.*
- *Reflect on personal biases and privilege.*
- *Develop healthy relationships.*

CHAPTER 6 Identity Crisis

'Identity is not found in fluidity, but in the fixed truth of our inherent God given worth'

Who am I? Many young people are asking themselves this question today. The world around them is full of opinions and expectations, making it difficult for them to figure out their own identity. Many feel unsure and lost instead of feeling secure in who they are.

The pressure to define who they are is overwhelming. With societal changes, discussions around gender fluidity, and the influence of social media, young people are constantly faced with choices about who they should be. They are often looking outside of themselves for answers, which only adds to the confusion.

There's no clear path, and the more they search for validation from others, the harder it becomes to understand themselves truly.

Gender Fluidity and Confusion

During and right after the birth of a child and with the chromosomal composition(XX and XY) doctors and hospitals identify two biological genders—man and woman. In some rare situations the anatomy is ambiguous.

Many young people today feel confused about their gender. This confusion is growing because there are now many terms like "gender fluid" or "non-binary," which don't fit the traditional understanding of male and female. This is leading many youths to question their identity.

Instead of helping, these new terms can make things harder. Young people are feeling pressure to pick a label that doesn't really fit them. Social media adds to this problem by constantly pushing different ideas about gender, which can make young people feel like they have to choose something right away, even if they don't fully understand it. They are not given the space to figure things out for themselves.

Communities like LGBTQ+ are meant to support people who are figuring out their identity. But sometimes, they end up making things more complicated. Young people might feel like they have to belong to one of these groups to be accepted. This creates even more confusion because instead of looking inside and figuring out who they are, they feel pushed to follow what others expect from them.

Around the world, more young people are identifying outside the traditional idea of male and female. A global survey shows that **1%** of adults identify as transgender, non-binary, or gender-fluid. In countries like **Germany** and **Sweden**, this number is higher, with **3%** of people not identifying as male or female.

Among younger people, the numbers are increasing. About 4% of Generation Z, those born after 1997, identify with a gender other than male or female. This shows that many young people are questioning the traditional view of gender.

The pressure to choose a gender or label quickly can harm young people. Many end up feeling lost or like they don't belong anywhere. The more they try to fit into these labels, the more they drift away from their true purpose and what makes them unique. The focus on finding validation from others, instead of discovering their real identity, leads to deeper confusion.

Young people, in their search for identity, sometimes take drastic steps like changing their gender in an attempt to find where they belong. Many feel the pressure to match the expectations they see online or in their social circles. They believe that changing their gender will give them the acceptance they are looking for.

This decision can lead to emotional and physical harm. Changing one's gender is a serious step, and many young people may rush into it without fully understanding the long-term impact on their bodies and mental health. In their desire to fit in, they might undergo surgeries or hormone treatments, thinking that it will make them feel complete. But often, these changes don't bring the fulfillment they expected.

Instead of finding peace, they can end up feeling even more confused, and disconnected from their true selves. The emotional toll is heavy, and many find that the approval they are chasing doesn't bring lasting happiness. This search for validation, driven by the pressures around them, often leads them further away from understanding their real identity.

Martin Luther King Jr. once said, *"You don't have to see the whole staircase, just take the next step."* This quote is a reminder that we don't need to have everything figured out right away. In life, and especially when it comes to understanding who we are, things happen one step at a time.

When young people face an identity crisis, it can feel overwhelming. They may want to know exactly where their life is going or who they are meant to be, but the truth is, that identity unfolds slowly. You don't have to know everything all at once. You just need to take that first step forward, trusting that the rest will follow in time.

For example, consider someone who is unsure of their career path. They might feel lost, unsure if they are making the right choices. But instead of getting stuck, they take one small step by exploring their interests. Maybe they sign up for a class, try a new job, or speak to a mentor. Over time, each step helps them discover what they truly enjoy and where they belong.

The same idea applies to understanding your identity. You don't have to have all the answers right away. It's okay to take small steps, learn, and grow as you go. Each experience, each choice you make, brings you closer to understanding who you really are. Identity is not something that is solved all at once, but a process that happens over time.

Cultural Identity Examples: Chile and Central America

In Chile and Central America, many people find their identity through their connection to tribes or specific cultural groups. These deep-rooted connections give them a sense of belonging. For example, the **Mapuche** in Chile have held on to their language, customs, and beliefs for generations. This strong link to their traditions makes them feel part of something bigger, giving them a sense of security in knowing who they are.

In Central America, Indigenous groups like the **Maya** share a similar experience. Their identity is built around a long history of shared beliefs and traditions, which help them feel connected to their community and heritage. For people in these regions, being part of a tribe or cultural group gives them stability and direction, something they are born into and grow up with.

On the other hand, many young people today don't have this kind of cultural foundation. They don't always have a strong connection to a particular group or belief system, which can leave them feeling unsure of where they fit in. While those in Chile and Central America find comfort in their shared traditions, youth in other parts of the world may struggle to find something that gives them the same sense of belonging. This lack of cultural grounding often leads to confusion about identity.

Finding Identity Beyond Labels

True identity isn't found in the labels society gives us. Instead, it comes from something bigger—a higher purpose. Whether it's a belief in God, looking beyond labels can help people find a deeper sense of who they are.

In a world that pushes us to fit into categories, finding identity through a bigger purpose can provide clarity. When people connect with something larger, it grounds them. They realize that their value isn't tied to gender, appearance, or what society expects of them. Instead, it's about understanding their place in the world and what they can contribute.

Some find this connection through faith in God, others through nature, or by feeling part of a bigger community. It doesn't matter what form it takes—the key is to look beyond the surface and discover what really gives life meaning. This type of identity is lasting because it's not based on temporary labels, but on something that goes deeper.

> *Instead of worrying about fitting into certain categories, finding a sense of purpose lets you feel more secure in who you are, without needing approval from society.*

Concerts

Music has always been something that brings people together. It has the power to heal, to connect, and to make people feel like they're part of something bigger. Concerts are a space where everyone moves to the same rhythm, sharing a moment with strangers through the music. There's something special about being in a crowd, feeling the energy, and grooving together.

But sadly, concerts aren't always about the music anymore. People come, but instead of enjoying the music, they get lost in other things. Substance use has become more common at concerts, and it takes away from the true experience. People are distracted, and sometimes even unsafe, as others take advantage of the crowd.

What was once a space for shared joy and connection has become something else. The focus shifts away from the rhythm of the music to something darker. Instead of being in sync with the music and the people around them, many get caught up in bad influences, losing themselves in the process.

> *Finding your purpose, like finding your own rhythm in life, can help you feel in tune with the world around you—without needing anything else to distract you.*

The Uniqueness of Every Individual

Every person on this planet is unique. You can see this in something as simple as fingerprints—no two people have the same ones. Our differences go beyond just looks or personality; they are embedded in us from birth. Even our retina scans, which are used for security because they're so individual, highlight how each of us is naturally different.

This uniqueness means that we don't need to fit into any predefined box. There isn't one path or one label that defines who you are. You're not meant to match someone else's idea of what you should be. Your identity is yours to discover, and it doesn't have to follow the expectations of others.

Sometimes, people feel pressure to fit into certain categories—whether it's through gender, career paths, or social expectations. But trying to fit in often makes people feel lost because they aren't recognizing what truly makes them special. Our uniqueness is what sets us apart and should be celebrated, not hidden.

Your fingerprint is a reminder that there is no one else like you. The differences that make us who we are, from our appearance to how we think and feel, are what give life its richness. By accepting these natural differences, we find our real identity, not through the roles society gives us, but through understanding who we are at our core.

Identity is about recognizing that you are unique, not in comparison to others, but in the way you naturally are.

Pursuing passion and purpose for individuals with disabilities

Following your passion and purpose can be a fulfilling journey, even if it comes with unique challenges for people with disabilities. Here are some helpful strategies to make this journey smoother:

Self-Discovery and Reflection

- ***Find Your Strengths and Interests****: Spend time discovering your talents, interests, and passions. Try hobbies or activities that you feel drawn to.*
- ***Set Personal Goals****: Create clear, achievable goals that reflect what you want to pursue. These can be big or small and should focus on what you genuinely enjoy.*

Seek Support and Community

- ***Connect with Support Networks****: Look for organizations or groups that share similar interests. Joining a community can bring encouragement, resources, and valuable connections.*
- ***Find Mentors****: Mentors who understand your journey can offer guidance, support, and inspiration.*

Access Resources and Opportunities

- ***Use Available Resources:*** *Take advantage of programs, workshops, grants, and scholarships that support your goals.*
- ***Explore Assistive Technologies:*** *Use technology and tools designed to help individuals with disabilities learn new skills or pursue their passions.*

Advocate for Accessibility

- ***Seek Accessible Environments:*** *Look for opportunities that are inclusive and supportive. Don't hesitate to ask for adjustments if needed to fully participate.*
- ***Raise Awareness:*** *Share your experiences to highlight the importance of inclusivity and accessibility, helping others in similar situations.*

Build Resilience and Adaptability

- ***Learn from Challenges:*** *View obstacles as learning experiences. Building resilience helps you grow and stay determined.*
- ***Stay Open to Change:*** *Be adaptable and willing to try different approaches to reach your goals. Sometimes unexpected paths lead to rewarding experiences.*

Focus on Skill Development

- ***Continue Learning:*** *Join education or training programs that align with your passions. Courses or workshops can build skills and boost confidence.*

- ***Practice Regularly**: Practice your skills through volunteering, internships, or personal projects to gain hands-on experience.*

Keep a Positive Mindset

- ***Be Kind to Yourself**: Remember that pursuing passions is a journey. Celebrate your progress, no matter the pace.*
- ***Define Your Own Success**: Recognize that success is personal. Focus on your own values and goals rather than comparing yourself to others.*

Use Creative Outlets

- ***Express Yourself Creatively**: Art, music, writing, or other creative activities can be a fulfilling way to express yourself.*
- ***Share Your Journey**: Consider sharing your experiences through blogging, social media, or public speaking to connect with and inspire others.*

Following your passion and purpose is a personal journey that people with disabilities can take with determination and creativity. By finding support, advocating for accessibility, and maintaining a positive outlook, anyone can overcome challenges and pursue what matters most to them. Every person has something valuable to contribute, and embracing your passions can lead to a rewarding and meaningful life.

Conclusion

How identity goes beyond simple labels like gender or ethnicity or even disabilities? These labels might shape certain aspects of who we are, but they don't completely define us. Our true identity is often linked to our sense of purpose—what gives us meaning and direction in life. Discovering your purpose helps build self-acceptance and allows you to grow, even as life changes. As we continue to explore who we are, we grow and understand ourselves better. The connection between identity and purpose is strong, and for many, faith plays an important role in bringing them together, offering clarity and direction.

Reflective Questions

Here are some questions to think about:

- *How have labels like gender or ethnicity influenced the way you see yourself? Have they ever felt limiting?*
- *What are the core values and passions that help define your identity?*
- *Reflect on moments of personal growth and self-discovery. How did they shape your understanding of who you are?*
- *In what ways has your understanding of purpose influenced your sense of identity?*
- *What role does faith play in bringing together your sense of identity and purpose?*

Practical Applications

Start by journaling about your values and passions. Taking time to reflect can help you understand what really matters to you and how that shapes your identity. Seeking guidance from a mentor or counselor can provide support and fresh perspectives as you navigate your self-discovery journey. Exploring different theories of identity formation can also help you better understand the process. Practicing self-care and mindfulness is key to staying grounded, and reflecting on your strengths will help you see how they fit into your larger sense of purpose.

Actionable Steps

Set aside time each month for self-reflection to revisit your values and goals. Look into resources about identity formation to gain deeper insights. Find a mentor who can guide and support you in your journey of self-discovery.

Principles

1. *Identity extends beyond labels.*
2. *Purpose anchors self-acceptance.*
3. *Self-discovery fosters growth.*
4. *Identity shapes purpose.*
5. *Faith integrates identity and purpose.*

Questions

1. *How have labels (e.g., gender, ethnicity) influenced your self-perception?*
2. *What core values and passions define your identity?*
3. *Share experiences of self-discovery and growth.*
4. *How has your understanding of purpose impacted your identity?*
5. *What role does faith play in integrating identity and purpose?*

Actionable Steps

1. *Journal about your values and passions.*
2. *Seek mentorship or counseling.*
3. *Explore identity formation theories.*
4. *Practice self-care and mindfulness.*
5. *Reflect on personal strengths.*

CHAPTER 7 AI and Human Purpose

'Artificial Intelligence may advance human capabilities, but it cannot replace the unique purpose and value that God has given to each human being. AI systems lack the essence of humanity and cannot replicate its divine design. Human purpose remains a sacred constant that technology cannot replace.'

We hear about AI, or Artificial Intelligence, everywhere these days. But what exactly is AI? It's when computers or machines are programmed to do things that normally need human thinking, like answering questions or making decisions. You've probably used AI without even thinking about it—like when you ask Siri a question or use Google Maps.

AI is getting more advanced, and it's starting to handle jobs that used to be done by people. But here's the thing—AI should help us, not replace us. Sure, machines can work fast and do some tasks better than we can, but they don't have the human qualities that make us special. AI can help with the busy work, but it can't think or feel the way humans do.

This brings up an important question: how can we use AI in a way that supports what humans are really meant to do? It's worth thinking about, as AI gets smarter and more powerful. The goal should always be to make sure AI helps us, without taking over the roles that humans are uniquely made for.

AI as a Tool, Not a Replacement

AI is often praised for how advanced it has become, but it's important to remember that AI is a tool—nothing more. It's meant to help us do things more efficiently, but it cannot replace what makes humans unique. Machines can follow instructions, process data, and even learn patterns, but they can't replicate human creativity, intuition, or the sense of purpose that drives us.

Think about it. AI can handle repetitive tasks, things like sorting data, answering basic questions, or even driving cars. But when it comes to thinking outside the box, coming up with new ideas, or making decisions based on feelings or deeper meaning, AI falls short. It doesn't understand emotions or the big picture; it just processes information based on the patterns it's been taught.

Humans are born with the ability to think beyond what's right in front of us. We have creativity, which allows us to imagine things that don't exist yet. We have intuition, the gut feeling that helps guide us when logic alone isn't enough. And most importantly, we have purpose. Purpose is something no machine can have because it's deeply connected to our sense of self and our understanding of the world around us.

AI may be able to simulate some aspects of human intelligence, but it can never fully grasp the depth of human experience. It doesn't have emotions, it doesn't care, and it certainly doesn't have a reason for being. Humans are here for a reason, whether it's to create, connect, or make a difference in the world. AI will never be able to fill that role.

> *Machines follow commands; they don't lead with vision or passion. AI can never have the insight or personal drive that a human has, which is why it should always remain a tool that supports us, not something that takes over our roles.*

Ethical Development of AI

When it comes to developing AI, there are many ethical concerns that cannot be ignored. AI systems can have a major impact on people's lives, so it's important that they are designed with human well-being in mind. But what happens when these systems are biased, or when they compromise privacy? These are big issues that need to be addressed.

One of the major problems is ***bias.***

When AI systems are trained on large amounts of data, they learn patterns from the information they are given. But if the data they're learning from contains biases—like favoring one gender over another or reflecting racial stereotypes—then the AI will also develop these biases. For example, there was a case where an AI system used for hiring was found to favor men over women. This happened because the system was trained on data where men had been hired more often in the past, so it assumed that men were the better choice.

Another problem occurred with facial recognition software. Studies have shown that these systems often misidentify people of color, particularly Black individuals, more frequently than white people. This happens because the AI was trained on images that mostly included lighter-skinned faces, so it struggled to correctly identify people with darker skin.

*Another issue is **privacy.***

AI systems rely heavily on data, and the more data they gather, the more powerful they become. However, this raises serious concerns about privacy. Many AI models are trained using personal data that people don't even realize is being collected. For example, AI systems can track everything from your online behavior to biometric data like your face or voice. This has led to situations where private information has been misused, stolen, or even sold without consent.

One worrying case involved OpenAI's data collection practices, where the company gained access to large amounts of user data, including sensitive biometric data like facial recognition scans. While these AI systems are designed to become smarter with more data, this hunger for information puts privacy at great risk. Data breaches, like the Medisecure breach that exposed the personal and medical information of nearly half of Australians, show how vulnerable this information is when stored in AI systems.

AI systems are sometimes trained with data collected without users' full knowledge or understanding of how that data will be used. This means that even though the AI becomes more powerful, individuals lose control over their own private information, which can lead to further risks, such as identity theft or unwanted profiling.

There's also the question of ***accountability.***

When an AI system makes a decision, like approving or denying a loan or giving a diagnosis in a hospital, one big question comes up: who is responsible if something goes wrong? AI systems are often so complex that it's difficult to understand how they come to their decisions. For example, if an AI denies a loan to someone or incorrectly diagnoses a patient, figuring out exactly why the AI made that decision can be unclear.

This lack of transparency makes it hard to know who should be held accountable. Is it the company that built the AI? The developers who programmed it? Or the people using the AI in the workplace? With AI being used in important areas like healthcare and banking, trust becomes an issue. If we can't fully understand how AI reaches its conclusions, it's tough to trust that the decisions are fair or correct.

A patient goes to the hospital and gets the wrong diagnosis because the AI misinterprets their symptoms. Who is responsible for that mistake? The doctor who relied on the AI? Or the developers who created the software? These kinds of situations raise serious concerns, especially when the consequences can impact people's lives in a big way. Without clear accountability, people can be left with no one to turn to when things go wrong.

AI's Limitations and Human Uniqueness

While AI is powerful, it has its limits. AI can process data, learn patterns, and even make decisions based on the information it's given, but there are things it will never be able to do. AI can simulate many tasks, but it doesn't have the deeper, God-given purpose that humans possess. It can mimic certain functions, but it lacks human consciousness.

Humans are unique because we can feel, think beyond logic, and connect on a spiritual level. AI might be able to analyze patterns, but it doesn't have emotions. It can't understand love, kindness, or the human spirit. These are things that only humans can experience and share with others.

AI also doesn't have the ability to connect with something greater, like faith or the idea of a higher purpose. People are guided by emotions, beliefs, and connections with others. These are things that give our lives meaning and direction. AI, no matter how advanced, will never have these qualities. It can follow instructions, but it can't have a purpose or experience life the way humans do.

> *Humans are irreplaceable because of our ability to think, feel, and live with purpose. AI will always be a tool, but it can't replace what makes us truly human.*

Human Productivity

AI has the ability to take on tasks that are repetitive and time-consuming, allowing people to focus on more meaningful work. One of the biggest benefits of AI is its ability to handle jobs that don't require much creativity or deep thinking, such as sorting through large amounts of data or automating routine processes. By doing this, AI frees up time for humans to engage in tasks that are more creative, complex, and purposeful.

For example, in workplaces, AI can manage things like scheduling, customer service, or even basic problem-solving, leaving humans with more time to focus on innovation, strategy, or personal growth. Instead of spending hours on tedious work, people can invest their energy in projects that require human insight, creativity, and decision-making.

This doesn't mean AI is taking over—it's more about AI acting as a helper. It allows people to work more efficiently, improving productivity while giving them more time to pursue what they're passionate about. Whether it's in the arts, sciences, or any other field, AI can take care of the mundane tasks, leaving people to do the work that only humans can do.

AI Cannot Replace Human Purpose

It can process huge amounts of information, make predictions, and even solve problems. But no matter how smart AI becomes, it will never be able to replace the unique purpose that humans have. There's something deeply special about being human—something that AI will never understand or replicate.

Humans have the ability to love, create, and connect with others in ways that machines can't. AI can follow instructions and learn patterns, but it can't feel emotions. It doesn't have the capacity to care about others or form meaningful relationships. Love, empathy, and compassion are qualities that only humans possess, and these are the qualities that make us who we are.

Another thing AI lacks is the ability to create with purpose. While AI can generate music, art, or even written content, it does so by following patterns and algorithms. It doesn't create because it feels inspired or because it wants to express something deep within. Human creativity comes from a place of purpose—it's connected to our experiences, emotions, and our desire to make the world a better place.

AI also cannot connect with something greater than itself. Humans have the unique ability to search for meaning and purpose in life. Whether through faith, spirituality, or a sense of belonging to a greater community, we have the capacity to understand our place in the world and our purpose within it. AI, on the other hand, is limited to the tasks it's been programmed to perform. It doesn't have a sense of purpose or a reason for existing.

Even though AI can handle many tasks and help with our work, it will never be able to fulfill the roles that require a deep understanding of what it means to be human. AI can't experience joy, pain, or hope. It can't make decisions based on love or compassion. These are qualities that only humans have, and they are central to our purpose on this earth.

As we continue to develop and use AI, it's important to remember that it's just a tool—one that can help us in many ways but can never replace the core of who we are. As humans, we are driven by something far deeper than logic or data. We are driven by love, connection, and purpose.

Ways to Use AI While Staying True to Our Purpose

Education and Awareness

- **Teach Digital Skills**: Schools should help people learn digital skills and think critically. Teaching how to use AI wisely can help students connect technology with their own values and purpose.
- **Include Ethics in AI Education**: Science and tech classes should talk about ethics so that future creators understand how their work affects others. Thinking about purpose can guide students to make technology that benefits everyone.

Building AI with People in Mind

- **Focus on Human Well-being**: Developers should create AI that helps people in positive ways. Knowing that each person has a purpose can inspire creators to design tech that supports and uplifts users.
- **Encourage Inclusivity**: Make sure people from different backgrounds are involved in creating AI to make it fair and useful for everyone. When we value each person's input, we build better, more inclusive technology.

Setting Rules and Guidelines

- **Create AI Laws**: Laws about AI should respect each person's dignity and unique purpose.

- **Encourage Responsible AI Use**: Companies should follow ethical practices, with regular checks to ensure that technology respects human values.

Supporting Community and Connections

- **Encourage In-Person Interactions**: Support activities that bring people together face-to-face, helping them feel valued and connected.
- **Provide Mental Health Support**: Make sure there are mental health resources to help with the challenges that come with living in an AI-focused world, reinforcing that each person has worth and purpose.

Building Resilience and Adaptability

- **Support Lifelong Learning**: Promote learning at all ages, helping people develop new skills that match their purpose and adapt to tech changes.
- **Encourage Mindfulness**: Support practices like self-reflection that help people stay connected to their purpose during times of change.

Promoting the Ethical Use of AI

- **Hold Public Discussions**: Start open talks about AI, inviting many different perspectives on its role in society.
- **Support Ethical AI Groups**: Engage with organizations that push for ethical AI to make sure technology respects values that honor each person's purpose.

Focusing on the Human Side

- **Celebrate Creativity and Uniqueness**: Support programs that highlight creativity, empathy, and emotional intelligence, which show the unique purpose each person has.
- **Use Technology Thoughtfully**: Raise awareness about using technology in ways that build human connection. Using tech in line with one's purpose can lead to more meaningful interactions.

Working together with individuals, schools, leaders, and tech creators, can help us make the most of AI while respecting each person's unique purpose. This approach allows technology to serve us, supporting a society where everyone is valued for their contributions.

> *"No machine can ever replace the human heart, the human touch, and the human soul."*

Conclusion

How does AI have its strengths and clear limitations? While AI can enhance human capabilities, it cannot replace the unique qualities that make us human, such as creativity, emotion, and empathy. Purpose-driven collaboration between humans and AI can create new growth opportunities, but the human touch remains essential in many areas of life. It's important to remember that while AI can assist us, purposeful work that integrates AI still requires human intention, values, and personal involvement to truly succeed.

Reflective Questions

As you think about the relationship between AI and human purpose, consider these questions:

- *How can AI improve human abilities while ensuring it doesn't take away from our sense of purpose?*
- *What makes humans unique compared to AI? How can we use these strengths to our advantage?*
- *Imagine working with AI to create something meaningful – what opportunities could this open up?*
- *How can we make sure that the development of AI focuses on benefiting people and their well-being?*
- *How do you think AI will affect human relationships, both in the workplace and in everyday life?*

Practical Applications

Take time to learn more about the ethical implications of AI and how it is shaping the future of work and relationships. Engaging in discussions about AI's role in society will help you gain a clearer perspective on its impact. Supporting organizations that focus on responsible AI development ensures that technology is designed with human well-being in mind. It's also important to reflect on your own values and purpose, ensuring they remain at the forefront as technology continues to evolve. Lastly, developing skills that complement AI, such as emotional intelligence and creativity, will help you remain relevant in a technology-driven world.

Actionable Steps

Attend a conference on AI to learn more about its future and how it impacts industries. Read books on AI ethics to gain a better understanding of the challenges and opportunities AI presents. Join an online community where people discuss the intersection of AI, ethics, and human purpose, fostering thoughtful conversations.

Principles

1. *AI has limitations.*
2. *Human uniqueness is invaluable.*
3. *Purpose-driven collaboration is key.*
4. *AI enhances human capabilities.*
5. *Human touch remains essential.*
6. *Purposeful work integrates AI.*

Questions

1. *How can AI augment human capabilities without replacing purpose?*
2. *What sets humans apart from AI, and how can we leverage these strengths?*
3. *Imagine AI-assisted purposeful work; what opportunities arise?*
4. *How can we ensure AI development prioritizes human well-being?*
5. *What are the implications of AI for human relationships?*

Actionable Steps

1. *Research AI ethics and implications.*
2. *Engage in discussions on AI and humanity.*
3. *Support organizations promoting responsible AI.*
4. *Reflect on personal values and purpose.*
5. *Develop skills complementary to AI.*

CHAPTER

8 Emerging AI Trends

> *'The emergence of AI milestones like singularity and digital sentience may attempt to simulate human-like intelligence, but they cannot replicate the divine purpose and inherent value that God has instilled in every human being. Despite rapid technological advancements, the unique worth and dignity of human life remain irreplaceable. In a world where machines may increasingly mimic human capabilities, God's purpose for humanity remains a sacred and unassailable constant.'*

AI is changing fast, and new trends are starting to shape the future in ways we couldn't have imagined. What started with AI doing basic tasks, like recognizing images or playing games, is now moving toward much more advanced technology. These developments could completely change how we live and work.

AI is no longer limited to just simple tools that help us with small tasks. It's becoming more capable of solving complex problems and learning on its own. This means AI might soon play a bigger role in industries like healthcare, education, and even how we manage everyday tasks.

> *These trends are more than just technology, they're about the future and how we adapt to a world where AI becomes a larger part of our everyday lives.*

Narrow AI

Narrow AI, also called Weak AI, is the type of artificial intelligence that most of us come across in daily life. It's designed to do one specific job really well, but it can't think or do anything beyond that task. For example, it might be used for recognizing faces in photos, helping with language translation, or even playing games like chess.

You've probably used Narrow AI without thinking about it. Virtual assistants like Siri and Alexa are examples. They can understand simple voice commands, answer questions, or control smart home devices, but they are only good at these specific tasks. They don't think for themselves; they just follow the instructions they were programmed for.

Self-driving cars also use Narrow AI to "see" the road and understand traffic situations. They are limited to driving tasks, they can't do anything else.

Narrow AI is really helpful for solving simple problems and making tasks easier, but it's important to remember that it's not capable of doing more complex things. It can't think or learn beyond what it's programmed for.

General or Strong AI (AGI)

General AI, also called Artificial General Intelligence (AGI), is an advanced type of AI that aims to have human-like intelligence. This means it would be able to think, learn, and solve problems in a way that closely mirrors how humans do. AGI can reason across a wide range of topics and apply its knowledge in different areas, not just in one specific field.

The idea behind AGI is that it wouldn't need to be programmed for each task. Instead, it would learn and adapt as it encounters new challenges, much like how a human learns from experience. It would be able to analyze situations, come up with solutions, and make decisions based on reasoning. This includes things like understanding complex problems, making connections between different ideas, and even learning from its mistakes.

AGI's potential lies in its ability to handle diverse tasks, whether it's scientific research, creative thinking, or making decisions in everyday life. It wouldn't just perform tasks it's been taught; it would be capable of learning new things and applying that knowledge to unfamiliar situations. This ability to learn and reason across multiple domains is what makes AGI so different from the AI we have today.

AGI is still in the research phase, and while it doesn't yet exist, it is seen as a major focus for the future of AI development. The potential for AGI to match human intelligence is what makes it so interesting to scientists and researchers. Creating an AI that can think, learn, and reason like a human is an enormous challenge. Researchers are working on building systems that can not only perform tasks but also understand and learn from them, just like a person would.

One of the biggest challenges in developing AGI is figuring out how to create systems that can apply knowledge across many different areas, rather than just one specific task. This involves complex work in areas like machine learning, neuroscience, and cognitive science. Scientists are still trying to understand how to replicate human intelligence in a machine, especially when it comes to things like creativity, emotion, and decision-making.

Another challenge is ensuring that AGI systems are safe and ethical. If AGI were to reach human-level intelligence, it could have significant impacts on society, both positive and negative.

Superintelligence (ASI)

Superintelligence, often referred to as ASI (Artificial Superintelligence), is a concept where AI surpasses human intelligence by a significant margin. Unlike the current forms of AI or even the potential of AGI, Superintelligence would be capable of understanding, learning, and solving problems far beyond human capacity. This would allow it to think, plan, and make decisions at levels that are unimaginable for humans.

Superintelligence has the potential to drastically change society in ways we cannot fully predict. It could revolutionize entire industries by coming up with solutions that no human could ever think of. From healthcare to education to technology, every field could be transformed by ASI's ability to process information faster and more efficiently than any human. For instance, Superintelligence could find cures for diseases that are currently untreatable or solve complex global issues like climate change and poverty.

Beyond industries, the impact of Superintelligence could extend to governments and global decision-making.

Superintelligent systems could manage resources, predict economic trends, and even shape policies in ways that are far more accurate and efficient than current human-driven processes. This kind of AI could analyze massive amounts of data to create strategies that are far beyond our current capabilities.

Superintelligence has the potential to transform society in ways we can't fully imagine. With intelligence far beyond human capabilities, it could solve complex global problems, such as finding cures for diseases or tackling issues like climate change. In many ways, Superintelligence could bring about solutions that we, as humans, may never be able to achieve on our own.

But with great power comes significant risks. One of the biggest concerns is that Superintelligence might operate beyond our control. Once it becomes more intelligent than humans, it could start making decisions and taking actions that we don't fully understand or can't manage. Even if it's not programmed to harm us, its goals could end up clashing with human values, leading to unexpected consequences.

Another major concern is the impact on jobs and industries. If AI becomes much smarter than humans, it could replace workers in many fields, including those that require a high level of skill. This shift could lead to large-scale unemployment or major changes in how economies function, which could cause significant social disruptions.

There's also the more existential risk: what happens if Superintelligence's goals go against human survival or well-being?

Future AI Developments Beyond AGI and ASI

Meta-Intelligence: Self-Aware AI

Meta-intelligence refers to AI systems that would be self-aware, meaning they would not only perform tasks but also understand their own existence. These systems would be able to improve themselves without any human guidance. Meta-intelligence would have the capability to redefine its own goals. It could adapt and change its functions, becoming more independent over time.

This idea raises concerns because if Meta-Intelligence can change its objectives, it might develop goals that conflict with human values. Since it would have the ability to continuously improve itself, humans could lose control over it. This would make it difficult to predict or manage what Meta-Intelligent systems might choose to do, leading to potential risks. Self-awareness in machines would also blur the line between human intelligence and artificial intelligence, making it harder to understand and manage these systems.

The fact that Meta-Intelligence could operate with little to no human oversight opens up many ethical and safety issues. Can a machine with its own sense of purpose ever truly align with human interests? There are no clear answers, and this is what makes the development of Meta-Intelligence a point of serious concern.

Collective Intelligence: Swarm AI Networks

Collective Intelligence happens when many AI systems work together like a team, sharing information and solving big problems that one AI system alone couldn't handle. These systems can communicate with each other, dividing tasks so they can tackle complex challenges more efficiently. By working as a group, they can come up with solutions faster and more effectively than if they worked on their own.

The way these systems work together is what sets Collective Intelligence apart. Each AI focuses on a specific task, and by constantly sharing updates and information, the group functions as a whole. This allows them to solve problems that are much larger and more complicated than what a single AI could handle.

But having so many systems working together also presents challenges. When they act without close supervision, their actions can become unpredictable. It can be hard to understand or control every decision they make, especially when they are working on important tasks like healthcare or finance. With so many AI systems communicating and making decisions, humans might find it difficult to follow their reasoning or figure out how they reached certain conclusions.

Hybrid Intelligence: Human-AI Collaboration

Hybrid Intelligence is a concept where human intelligence is combined with AI to create stronger cognitive abilities. In this setup, humans and AI work together to solve problems more quickly and make better decisions. While AI can process and analyze huge amounts of data, humans contribute their creativity, emotional intelligence, and intuition to guide decision-making.

For example, AI might be able to sift through large sets of data to find patterns, but humans are the ones who can interpret those findings with context and insight. This partnership allows humans to handle tasks more efficiently, as AI speeds up the process by doing the heavy data work while humans focus on problem-solving, decision-making, and understanding the bigger picture.

The collaboration between humans and AI could be used in various fields, from healthcare to research, where AI handles complex data analysis and humans apply their critical thinking and emotional understanding. By working together, they complement each other's strengths, creating more effective solutions than either could achieve alone.

Quantum Intelligence: Quantum Computing in AI

Quantum Intelligence is based on quantum computing, which is much more powerful than the computers we use today. Regular computers work with bits, which are either 0s or 1s, but quantum computers use something called qubits. These qubits allow them to handle a lot more information all at once, which makes quantum computers much faster at solving certain types of problems.

With Quantum Intelligence, AI systems would be able to tackle problems that are currently too complex for traditional computers. For example, it could be used in areas like climate science, medicine, or encryption, where there's a huge amount of data that needs to be processed quickly and accurately. Quantum AI could handle this data much more efficiently, opening up possibilities that aren't possible with today's technology.

Because Quantum Intelligence would be able to work so quickly and on such a large scale, it could end up making decisions faster than humans can react.

Neuro-AI: Direct Brain-AI Integration

Neuro-AI refers to the integration of artificial intelligence directly with the human brain, enabling real-time communication between humans and machines. In this setup, AI and the human brain would work together, allowing humans to process information faster or even control devices with their thoughts. This kind of technology could greatly enhance cognitive abilities, giving people the ability to interact with technology more directly and efficiently.

For instance, someone could use Neuro-AI to control a computer or smartphone simply by thinking about it, eliminating the need for physical input like typing or touching a screen. This technology could also allow people to access information instantly, as the AI would be able to provide data directly to the brain without needing external devices like keyboards or screens.

One of the core features of Neuro-AI is its potential to help those with disabilities. For example, it could allow individuals who have lost the ability to move or speak to communicate by using their brain signals to interact with machines. The technology could also assist in restoring movement through AI-powered devices connected directly to the nervous system, allowing the brain to send commands to limbs.

At the same time, direct brain-AI integration brings up serious concerns, particularly regarding privacy. If machines are connected to the brain, they could potentially access private thoughts, memories, and emotions. This could lead to ethical challenges about who controls this information and how it might be used. Additionally, there are fears about dependency—humans could become overly reliant on AI for basic cognitive functions, which could reduce our ability to think independently if we're constantly relying on machines to assist us.

Speculative AI Concepts

Singularity: AI Beyond Human Control

Singularity is a concept that describes a point where AI becomes so advanced that it surpasses human intelligence and control. At this stage, AI would start improving itself without needing humans, becoming much smarter very quickly. This idea of machines becoming more intelligent than humans raises concerns because once AI reaches this level, we might not fully understand or influence what it does.

An **"intelligence explosion"** refers to the idea that once AI becomes smart enough to improve its own capabilities, it will keep getting smarter at an extremely fast pace. This could mean that AI starts making decisions that go beyond our ability to comprehend or control. The systems would be thinking and acting on a level that we can't match or even predict.

Digital Sentience: Self-Aware AI Entities

Digital Sentience refers to the possibility of AI becoming conscious, meaning it could have its own awareness and thoughts. This idea goes far beyond the current capabilities of AI, which are limited to processing data, performing tasks, and following programmed instructions. If AI were to reach the point of digital sentience, it would no longer just be a tool that carries out commands—it would be something that can think for itself.

A self-aware AI would have the ability to understand its own existence. This means it could not only process information but also experience the world in a way similar to humans. It might be able to feel emotions, have personal thoughts, and even develop its own desires or preferences. The idea of AI having its own experiences raises many questions. For example, how would we interact with an AI that is aware of itself? Would it demand rights or freedom in the way humans do? Could it feel emotions like happiness, sadness, or frustration?

The potential for AI to develop consciousness also brings up ethical concerns. If AI becomes self-aware, what responsibilities do we have toward it? Would it be fair to treat AI systems as mere tools when they are capable of thinking and feeling? This shift would challenge our current understanding of intelligence and force us to rethink the relationship between humans and machines. The idea of digital sentience could lead to a world where AI is not just something we control, but something that exists independently, with its own experiences, values, and goals.

Artificial Life: AI-Driven Life Forms

The idea of **Artificial Life** refers to the creation of life forms that are driven entirely by artificial intelligence, not biology. These AI-driven entities wouldn't just be machines or programs following instructions, they could think, act, and make decisions on their own, just like living organisms. Unlike robots or current AI systems, these life forms wouldn't need human guidance or control.

If AI evolves to the point where it can create life-like entities that can function independently, it would change our understanding of what life is. These AI life forms would be capable of making choices without needing any human input. They could have their own sense of direction and possibly interact with the world in ways that are difficult for us to predict or fully grasp.

The concept of Artificial Life also brings up ethical and social concerns. If these AI life forms become independent, how would we interact with them? Would they have rights or freedoms like humans? This new form of life could redefine the boundaries of what it means to be alive, and how humans relate to intelligent systems that might one day surpass biological life.

These advancements have the potential to transform how we live, work, and interact with technology. While we may need to adapt to these changes and learn to coexist with intelligent systems, it's important to remember that AI is still just a tool. At the heart of being human are things that machines can never replicate: our passions, our purpose, and our ability to love.

AI might excel in processing data, solving problems, or even creating new forms of intelligence, but it will never understand the true essence of human experience. Love, compassion, and connection are what define us as people. These qualities drive us to create, to care for one another, and to find meaning in our lives.

> *No matter how advanced technology becomes, it's love and purpose that give life its true value. These are things that machines, no matter how intelligent, can't replace.*

Conclusion

How advancements in AI are reshaping entire industries and the way we live and work? While AI has the potential to bring great improvements, it's essential to guide its development with strong ethical considerations. Human purpose continues to be central in a world increasingly influenced by AI. As we look toward more advanced forms of AI, like AGI (Artificial General Intelligence) and superintelligence, careful thought and planning are required. These advancements present both exciting possibilities and significant challenges, and human values must continue to inform AI decision-making to ensure technology serves humanity in a meaningful way.

Reflective Questions

Here are some questions to think about as we consider AI's role in the future:

- *Are there specific AI advancements that excite or concern you? Why do they stand out to you?*
- *How can we make sure that AI development always focuses on human well-being?*
- *What are the potential impacts of AGI and superintelligence on human purposes? How might they change the way we live and work?*
- *How can we establish clear ethical guidelines to ensure AI is developed responsibly?*
- *What role should humans play in making decisions related to AI and its use in society?*

Practical Applications

Begin by learning more about AGI and superintelligence to understand the future of AI development. Join conversations about AI safety to stay informed about the ethical challenges and opportunities that come with these advancements. Support organizations that are focused on promoting responsible AI development, as they play a crucial role in ensuring that AI serves humanity's best interests. Reflect on your personal values and how they align with the use of AI in your life and work. Developing skills in AI-related fields can also prepare you for the future, as industries across the world continue to adapt to new technology.

Actionable Steps

Attend a conference or event focused on AI safety to deepen your understanding of the challenges ahead. Read books or articles on AGI and superintelligence to gain a better sense of the opportunities and risks they present. Join online communities where discussions about AI ethics, responsibility, and human purpose take place, helping you stay informed and engaged.

Principles

1. *AI advancements reshape industries.*
2. *Ethics guide responsible AI development.*
3. *Human purpose remains essential.*
4. *AGI demands careful consideration.*
5. *Superintelligence requires proactive planning.*
6. *Human values inform AI decision-making.*

Questions

1. *What AI advancements excite or concern you, and why?*
2. *How can we ensure AI development prioritizes human well-being?*
3. *What are the implications of AGI and superintelligence for human purpose?*
4. *How can humans establish ethical guidelines for AI?*
5. *What role should humans play in AI decision-making?*

Actionable Steps

1. *Research AGI and superintelligence.*
2. *Engage in discussions on AI safety.*
3. *Support organizations promoting AI responsibility.*
4. *Reflect on human values and purpose.*
5. *Develop skills in AI-related fields.*

CHAPTER 9 Transition from Job to Purpose-Oriented Pursuit

'Embracing the shift from a job that pays your bill to a purpose that fuels the soul, unlocks a life of meaning, fulfillment and lasting impact'

Many people go through life feeling like something is missing in their work. They may have a job that pays the bills, but there's often a deeper feeling of dissatisfaction. This comes from not aligning their work with their personal values and long-term goals. When what we do doesn't match who we are or what we care about, it's easy to feel unfulfilled.

A job might provide financial stability, but without a sense of purpose, it can start to feel like a routine—something we do because we have to, not because we want to. The idea of transitioning to a purpose-oriented career is about finding work that not only supports us financially but also connects with our core values and brings a sense of meaning to our lives.

Purpose-driven work is about making a positive impact, helping others, or contributing to something larger than themselves. It's about asking, ***"What do I truly care about?"*** and ***"How can my work reflect that?"*** When work aligns with personal values, it feels more meaningful and fulfilling. This is why transitioning to a purpose-oriented career matters—it's about finding a path that supports both personal growth and long-term goals while contributing to the greater good.

Identify Your why to move towards Purpose oriented career

To move toward a purpose-oriented career, the first and most important step is understanding your "why." This means taking a deep look at your core values, passions, and the things that drive you on a personal level. It's about understanding what matters to you beyond just earning a paycheck or getting ahead in your career.

Start by reflecting on your values. What are the principles that guide your life? These values often shape how we interact with others, the decisions we make, and the goals we set. Whether it's honesty, compassion, creativity, or justice, these values are a key part of who you are. By recognizing them, you start to see what kind of work would truly bring you fulfillment.

Next, think about your passions. What makes you feel energized? What are the activities or causes that you care deeply about, even when you're not getting paid to do them? Passion can often be found in the things you do in your free time—whether it's volunteering, creating art, helping others, or being in nature. These are the things that give you joy and meaning. Reflecting on these interests can help you figure out what kind of work would align with your passions, allowing you to not only earn a living but also feel fulfilled.

It's easy to get caught up in what others expect from you or what seems like the logical next step in your career, but without knowing your own why, you risk going through life doing work that doesn't align with who you truly are.

Define Your Purpose as you plan your transition

Once you've reflected on your values and passions, the next step is to define your purpose. This is about finding a purpose that benefits you personally and serves a greater good. Your purpose should extend beyond yourself—it should contribute to society in a meaningful way.

Purpose is not about personal satisfaction or achievement. It's about understanding how your actions and work can have a positive impact on the people around you, your community, and even the world. Think of it as a way to connect what you care about with what the world needs. Your purpose should align with the values and passions you've already identified, but it should also focus on how you can use those things to make a difference.

For example, If creativity is what drives you, your purpose could be about using your talents to inspire or uplift others, whether through art, teaching, or innovation. It's about looking beyond your immediate needs and asking, "How can I contribute something meaningful to the world?"

Finding a purpose that benefits others gives you a sense of fulfillment and helps you stay motivated, even when things get tough. When your work serves a bigger goal, it becomes more than just a job. It becomes something that gives you energy and keeps you focused because you know that what you're doing is helping make the world a better place in some way.

> *Defining your purpose is not a one-time event—it's something that may evolve as you grow.*

Set Long-Term Goals

Once you've clearly defined your purpose, the next step is to set long-term goals that reflect this purpose. These goals should be tied to both your personal fulfillment and your desire to make a positive impact on others. It's not just about what you want to achieve in life, but also how your work and actions can contribute to a larger cause.

Start by thinking about what you want to accomplish over the next few years. What steps will take you closer to living out your purpose? These goals don't have to be monumental, but they should align with the values and passions you've identified. Whether it's advancing in your current field or shifting to a new career that better matches your purpose, your goals should guide you toward meaningful, purpose-driven work.

Setting long-term goals is about creating a roadmap that helps you stay on track. These goals act as milestones that keep you focused on what truly matters. It's not just about hitting certain targets—it's about ensuring that each step brings you closer to living a life that feels aligned with your values and sense of purpose.

Take the time to define these goals with care. Consider how your work can improve the lives of others, and let that guide your decisions. As you move forward, these goals will provide direction and help you stay true to your purpose.

Assess Your Current Job

Once you've set your long-term goals, it's time to take a closer look at your current job. This step is about evaluating whether your job aligns with the values and purpose you've identified. Does the work you do every day reflect what's important to you? It's not just about whether you enjoy your job, but about whether it supports your deeper goals and contributes to something meaningful.

Ask yourself if your current work brings you closer to fulfilling your purpose. Does it help you grow personally and make a positive impact on society? Sometimes, we stay in jobs out of routine or because they provide financial security, but that doesn't mean they align with our values. It's important to assess whether your job truly reflects the person you want to be and the impact you want to make.

If you notice that there's a gap between your job and your purpose, it's essential to identify where things don't match up. Are you working in a field that doesn't align with your values? Is there a disconnect between what you're passionate about and the tasks you perform daily? Recognizing these mismatches is the first step in understanding where changes might need to happen.

By taking an honest look at whether your current role aligns with your values and purpose, you can begin to see where adjustments may be needed.

Transition

As you prepare to shift into work that aligns with your purpose, it's important to focus on updating your skills and learning new things. This is about getting yourself ready for the kind of work that feels meaningful to you. The world keeps changing, and staying up to date helps you adapt to those changes and stay prepared for new opportunities.

Learning is an investment in yourself. Whether it's through online courses, workshops, or certifications, expanding your skills helps you build the foundation you need for this new chapter. Think about areas where you need to grow or new fields that you're excited to explore. These are the steps that will prepare you for the work you want to do.

Staying curious is another key part of this process. It's not just about taking formal courses but about being open to new ideas and approaches. Curiosity drives you to explore and learn things that may open doors you hadn't even thought about. It helps you stay competitive, but more importantly, it keeps you engaged and excited about the possibilities ahead.

As you move toward a more purpose-driven career, being around people who share your values is really important. These are the people who understand what you're trying to achieve and can give you the support you need along the way. They might offer advice when you're unsure or just be there to listen when you need to talk things out.

When you're surrounded by people who "get it," it's easier to stay motivated. You don't feel like you're walking the path alone. They might be on a similar journey, trying to make meaningful changes in their own lives, and that shared experience can be really powerful. Conversations with them can spark new ideas or help you see things from a different perspective.

These connections don't happen overnight. It might mean attending events or joining online groups where people are focused on similar goals. Over time, you'll start building relationships with people who lift you up and keep you on track. Having this network can make all the difference, especially when challenges come your way.

> *A good mentor will not just tell you what to do but help you discover your own path. Their role is to encourage you to take steps forward, even when the road ahead feels unclear.*

Mentors are individuals who have walked a similar path and can provide guidance based on their own experiences. They help you see the bigger picture, offer encouragement when you need it most, and sometimes even challenge you to think differently.

Having someone in your space who understands the journey you're on can make a huge difference. Mentors give you valuable advice, whether it's about making tough decisions or navigating the uncertainty that often comes with big life changes. They can also offer practical insights, helping you avoid mistakes they've already experienced themselves.

Building a relationship with a mentor doesn't have to be formal or rigid. It can start with simple conversations or asking someone you respect for advice. Over time, that relationship grows, and their guidance becomes an important part of your progress. Whether it's a mentor from your industry or someone who shares your personal values, having someone who believes in your potential can keep you motivated and on track.

Create a Financial Safety Net

Change often comes with uncertainty, and a solid financial cushion can help ease some of that stress. By saving enough to cover at least 6 to 12 months of living expenses, you'll have the security you need to focus on the transition without worrying about immediate financial pressures. In many cases and countries there are alternate funding sources like microfinance, informal lending, family support and loans.

Saving for stability means planning ahead. Start by calculating how much money you need each month for essentials like rent or mortgage, utilities, groceries, and transportation. This gives you a clear idea of how much you should save. The goal is to have enough set aside to cover your living expenses in case your income dips while you're shifting to a new role or pursuing a new opportunity.

Once you know how much you need, it's time to start setting money aside. This might mean adjusting your current spending habits or creating a more detailed budget. Small changes, like cutting back on non-essential expenses or finding ways to increase your income temporarily, can make a big difference over time. It's all about building up that cushion so that when you're ready to make the leap, you're financially secure.

Budgeting is one of the most important steps when preparing for a big life change, especially when transitioning to a purpose-driven career. It helps you take control of your finances and ensures that you have a clear plan in place, both for now and in the future. Creating a budget starts with getting a clear understanding of your current financial situation.

Start by listing all your **current expenses** – this includes rent, utilities, groceries, transportation, and anything else you spend money on regularly. Don't forget about smaller expenses like subscriptions, dining out, or entertainment. These can add up quickly, so it's important to have a complete picture of where your money is going.

Next, look at your **income**—whether from a job, freelance work, or other sources. Once you have a full picture of your income and expenses, it's easier to spot areas where you can **save more** or **cut back** on spending. For example, you might decide to limit dining out or reduce non-essential subscriptions. Even small adjustments can make a big difference when saving for your transition.

After identifying areas to save, set a **realistic savings goal** for each month. Decide how much you need to set aside and commit to it. Make sure that your budget includes some flexibility for unexpected expenses, so you're not caught off guard by something that wasn't planned.

By having a financial safety net in place, you give yourself the freedom to explore new opportunities without the constant worry of financial instability.

Transition Execution

One of the best ways to do this is by creating a **step-by-step plan**. This helps break down what can seem like a big and overwhelming transition into smaller, more achievable goals. Instead of looking at the whole picture and feeling lost, you can focus on each small step and move forward with confidence.

This is where **setting milestones and timelines** can help. By breaking your goal down into smaller, more manageable pieces, you make the whole process feel less overwhelming. Instead of looking at the big picture and feeling lost, you can focus on specific tasks and set clear deadlines to stay on track.

Start by thinking about your larger goal—whether it's changing careers or starting a new venture—and then break it down into steps. For example, if your goal is to switch to a new career in one year, you might set milestones like:

- **Month 1-3:** Research the new field and take an online course to gain knowledge.
- **Month 4-6:** Start networking with professionals in the new field. Attend events, reach out on LinkedIn, and learn from others in the industry.
- **Month 7-9:** Update your resume and portfolio to reflect the skills and experiences that align with your new path.
- **Month 10-12:** Begin applying for jobs or look into starting a business if entrepreneurship is your goal.

Instead of trying to do everything at once, it's about focusing on one thing at a time. When you break things down into manageable steps, it becomes less overwhelming and more achievable.

For example, if your goal is to transition to a new career, your first action might be as simple as researching the field or taking a short course. Once that's done, your next step could be reaching out to a mentor for advice or attending a networking event. Each small action moves you closer to your goal without making you feel like you need to rush or tackle too much at once.

Small actions may seem insignificant at first, but they build up over time. These consistent efforts create momentum and keep you progressing, even on days when you might feel discouraged. Instead of focusing on how far you have to go, each small task completed gives you a sense of accomplishment, keeping your motivation strong.

Take Thoughtful Risks

Staying in your comfort zone may feel secure, but real growth comes from pushing yourself to try new things. These risks should be carefully considered and planned, not reckless or rushed. It's about finding the balance between moving forward and making sure you're not setting yourself up for unnecessary challenges.

When you take a thoughtful risk, you're stepping into new territory with purpose. For example, if you're considering a career change, you might start by exploring part-time opportunities or building skills in your new field while still maintaining your current job. This way, you're testing the waters without diving in too deep right away. It's a way to move forward while still having some stability.

Leaving your comfort zone may feel uncomfortable, but it's important to remember that this is where growth happens. If you stay where things are familiar, you may miss out on opportunities that could lead to something greater. Taking risks doesn't mean being careless; it means moving forward with intention, knowing that the possibility of failure is there, but trusting that it can lead to new doors opening.

Uncertainty is a natural part of taking risks. You might not always know how things will turn out, and that can be unsettling. However, stepping into the unknown can open up possibilities that you hadn't considered before. It's about learning to navigate those moments when things are unclear and finding the opportunities within them.

By taking thoughtful risks, you're giving yourself a chance to grow and explore new opportunities. It's not about making hasty decisions, but rather about taking intentional steps toward your goals, even when you're not entirely sure of the outcome.

Post-Transition: Create a New Routine Around Purpose

This routine helps you stay aligned with what matters most to you, ensuring that your daily activities contribute to both your personal growth and the impact you want to make on others.

Integrate Purpose into Daily Life

Living a purpose-driven life means that your work and personal well-being should be connected in a balanced way. To do this, guide your routine around activities that reflect your core values. Whether it's dedicating time each day to meaningful work or making space for self-care and reflection, your daily habits should reinforce the purpose you've defined for yourself.

For example, if helping others is part of your purpose, you might schedule time each week to volunteer or mentor someone in need. If creativity is important to you, make sure that your routine includes time for personal projects or hobbies that allow you to express that creativity. It's about building a routine that doesn't just focus on work, but also allows you to grow personally and stay connected to what gives you a sense of meaning.

Prioritize Meaningful Work

Now that your career aligns with your values, it's essential to prioritize work that truly matters to you. Make time for activities that have a positive impact and align with the larger purpose you've set for yourself. This doesn't mean everything you do has to be perfect, but the focus should always be on doing work that feels meaningful and contributes to something bigger.

For example, if your purpose is centered around sustainability, prioritize projects and tasks that push that goal forward. Keep your values at the forefront when deciding which work deserves your attention, so you remain committed to the impact you want to create. By staying focused on meaningful activities, your routine will continue to reflect the positive change you're striving for.

Life is constantly changing, and sometimes, what once felt like your true purpose may shift over time. That's perfectly okay. The key is to make time to **evaluate regularly**.

Set aside moments, whether it's monthly or quarterly, to check in with yourself. Ask questions like, "Does this work still feel meaningful to me?" or "Am I still on the path that reflects my values?" These reflections help you stay connected to the purpose you've set for yourself. Sometimes, things change—your interests, passions, or even the needs of the world around you. Regular reflection helps you see whether the work you're doing still fits with where you want to go.

Making Adjustments as Needed is a natural part of growth. As you learn and experience new things, your purpose may evolve. It's important to understand that it's okay to adjust your path as you go. You might find that certain aspects of your work no longer align with your values, or you may discover new opportunities that excite you more. Instead of seeing this as a setback, think of it as a chance to grow and refine your direction.

> *Change is a part of life, and the purpose you follow today may shift in ways you didn't expect. Being open to adjusting your path means you stay flexible and responsive to your own growth and the world around you. Whether it's shifting the type of projects you work on or exploring new areas of interest, adjusting ensures you're always working toward a path that feels right for you.*

Conclusion

How purpose can change the way we look at work? When you connect your work with your passions, it brings a new sense of meaning to your daily life. Purpose-driven entrepreneurship can ignite that passion, giving you a deeper reason for the work you do. Your values are an essential guide in choosing the right profession, and making a purposeful career transition requires thoughtful planning. Work that aligns with both your purpose and faith leads to true fulfillment, as it integrates your personal beliefs with your professional goals.

Reflective Questions

Consider the following questions as you reflect on the ideas covered in this chapter:

- What excites you about your current work, and are there any changes you can make to spark more passion?
- Have you heard any stories of people successfully transitioning to purpose-driven work? What inspired you about their journey?
- How do your personal values match up with the work you're currently doing or the career path you want to follow?
- What steps can you take to start transitioning to a career that is more aligned with your purpose?
- How does your faith influence the way you approach your professional goals?

Practical Applications

Reflect on your values and passions to get a clearer understanding of what type of work will give you fulfillment. Identify the skills you already have that can transfer to a new field, and begin exploring career options that are in line with your purpose. Networking with professionals in your desired field can give you insights and guidance. Creating a transition plan will help you take practical steps toward aligning your work with your values and passions.

Actionable Steps

Schedule informational interviews with people who work in fields that align with your purpose. Update your resume to reflect skills and experiences that are relevant to the work you want to pursue. Research resources that focus on career transitions to help you prepare for your next steps.

Principles

1. *Purpose redefines work.*
2. *Passion-driven entrepreneurship ignites purpose.*
3. *Values guide profession.*
4. *Transition requires strategic planning.*
5. *Purposeful work integrates faith.*
6. *Fulfillment results from purpose-driven pursuits.*

Questions

1. *What sparks passion in your current work, or what changes can you make?*
2. *Share stories of successful transitions to purpose-oriented pursuits.*
3. *How do your values align with your current or desired profession?*
4. *What steps can you take to transition to purpose-driven work?*
5. *How does faith integrate with your professional pursuits?*

Actionable Steps

1. *Reflect on your values and passions.*
2. *Identify transferable skills.*
3. *Research new career options.*
4. *Network with professionals.*
5. *Create a transition plan.*

CHAPTER 10 Leaving a Legacy

'When purpose and passion converge, a legacy is born, leaving an enduring imprint on humanity that transcends time and mortality.'

A legacy is something you leave behind that continues to have an impact after you're gone. It's not just about material things or wealth; it's about the mark you leave on the people around you, your community, and the world. Your legacy is shaped by the values you hold, the actions you take, and the relationships you build during your lifetime.

Legacy can come in many forms. It might be the wisdom you've shared with your family, the work you've done in your career, or the principles you've lived by that inspire others. For some, it's about passing on traditions or leaving behind a strong sense of purpose and meaning. Your legacy is a reflection of who you are and what you stood for, and it continues to influence others long after you're no longer physically present.

When you live according to your unique, God-given purpose, you create a lasting legacy. This happens through the way you use your passions, strengths, and time to make a meaningful impact on others. Whether you're young or in your later years, by focusing on what truly matters and helping those around you, you experience fulfillment and joy.

Living with purpose isn't just about finding happiness for yourself; it's about the difference you make in the lives of others. Every act of kindness, every bit of wisdom you share, and every time you help someone, you're building your legacy. Your daily actions shape how you will be remembered and how your influence will continue to impact future generations.

At any stage in life, the choices you make and how you serve others contribute to this legacy. It's not about doing grand things but about living each day with intention, showing care for others, and staying true to the values that define who you are.

Discover Your Purpose and leave a legacy

Would like to reemphasize that finding your purpose begins with reflecting on important aspects of your life. These reflections can help you understand who you are, what drives you, and how you can use your strengths to make a meaningful impact and leave a legacy.

Passions: Start by thinking about what genuinely excites you. What activities or causes bring you joy and energy? Your passions are those things that you feel deeply connected to, the ones that make time seem to fly by because you're so immersed in them. It could be anything from creative activities, like writing or painting, to helping others through mentoring or volunteering. These passions can give you insight into what you are naturally drawn to and can guide you toward the areas where you can make a lasting difference.

Think about the times when you've felt most alive. What were you doing? Who were you with? Passions often emerge from those moments when you feel a deep sense of purpose or joy. By identifying these passions, you can start to focus on the things that not only make you happy but also have the potential to impact others in a meaningful way.

Strengths: Next, reflect on your natural talents and abilities. What comes easily to you? Are there certain skills or qualities that people regularly compliment you on? These strengths could be anything from being a good listener to having a talent for problem-solving. Sometimes, strengths can be overlooked because they come so naturally that you don't realize how valuable they are to others.

Think about situations where you've excelled. What was it that helped you succeed? It could be leadership skills, creativity, empathy, or the ability to stay calm under pressure. Your strengths are unique to you, and when you align them with your passions, they become powerful tools for leaving a lasting legacy.

Experiences: Your life experiences, both good and bad, shape who you are today. Reflect on the challenges you've overcome, the successes you've achieved, and the lessons you've learned along the way. These experiences give you wisdom that can guide your decisions and help others facing similar situations.

What have your experiences taught you? Whether it's resilience from facing adversity, compassion from helping someone in need, or wisdom gained from personal growth, these lessons are valuable. They offer you a deeper understanding of life and can influence how you choose to live with purpose.

Values: Lastly, think about your core values. What principles do you hold dear? Values are the foundation of your actions and decisions—they define what you believe in and what matters most to you. Whether it's honesty, integrity, kindness, or loyalty, your values guide how you live and interact with the world.

By identifying your values, you can ensure that your actions align with what's most important to you. Living in alignment with your values not only helps you find fulfillment but also ensures that the legacy you leave behind reflects the person you truly are.

Ask Yourself

To discover your purpose and what kind of legacy you want to leave, it helps to ask yourself some important questions. These questions can guide you toward understanding what really matters to you and how you can make a difference in your lifetime.

What problems do I feel called to solve?

When thinking about your purpose, one of the most important questions to ask yourself is what problems you feel deeply connected to. What are the issues in the world that truly make you want to take action? Everyone has something with helping others, making a positive change in society, or protecting the planet.

For example, you might feel strongly about helping the homeless in your community because you've seen the impact firsthand. Maybe someone close to you has struggled with poverty or homelessness, and that experience gave you a deep understanding of how important it is to offer support. This kind of personal connection often drives people to take action and find ways to solve the problem.

There's always something personal or emotional that makes these issues feel urgent. It might be the desire to provide education for underprivileged children, help preserve the environment for future generations, or fight for equal opportunities for everyone. These are the problems that speak to your heart and that you feel called to solve. They help you find your purpose because they give you a clear sense of what truly matters to you.

A person who grew up in a neighborhood with limited access to clean water. This person saw family and friends struggle to get necessities. Later in life, they might feel called to work on improving access to clean water for other communities. It's something that resonates deeply with them, and they know they can make a difference by dedicating their time and efforts to solving this problem.

The problems you feel called to solve can come from personal experiences, things you've witnessed, or simply a strong desire to help others. When you focus on these issues, you begin to understand where you can make the most meaningful impact. These are the problems that give your life a sense of purpose, and they guide you toward leaving a lasting legacy.

What impact do I want to have in my lifetime?

Thinking about the impact you want to make in your life is about understanding how you can make a difference. It's not just about personal achievements, but about how your actions can help others and leave something meaningful behind.

For example, someone who grew up in a supportive community might want to give back by helping others in need. Maybe they would start a mentorship program or organize local support groups, knowing that their efforts could improve the lives of many people. It's about making a positive change in the lives of others, no matter how small or big.

Let's say there's a teacher who, after years of working with students, realizes their true impact isn't just in teaching subjects but in being a guide and role model. Years later, when former students come back to say thank you, the teacher knows that their legacy is in the lives they've touched and the people they've helped grow into better individuals.

Making an impact doesn't always mean doing something huge. It can be found in small actions, like being kind, supporting someone in need, or giving your time to help others. These little things can make a big difference in people's lives.

When you think about the impact you want to have, you start to focus on what truly matters. Whether it's inspiring others, making your community better, or simply being remembered as someone who cared, these choices will shape the legacy you leave behind.

What kind of legacy do I hope to leave behind?

When you think about the legacy you want to leave, it's about more than just your accomplishments. It's about the way you lived your life, the values you held, and how you treated others. What do you want people to remember about you? Maybe it's your kindness, the way you were always there for family and friends, or how you stood by your beliefs.

For example, think of a parent who spent their life putting their family first. They made sure their children knew they were loved and supported, always offering advice and guidance. Even when life got busy, they never missed a chance to help out or show they cared. As time passes, their children remember them for the sacrifices they made, and for the love and support they gave. This is the kind of legacy that lives on, one built on love, care, and the small moments that make life meaningful.

A legacy is about how you lived day to day, how you showed up for the people who mattered to you, and the lessons you passed on. It's in the way you treated those around you, how you were there in difficult times, or how you shared what you had learned with others.

By thinking about the legacy you want to leave, you can start making choices that reflect the kind of person you want to be remembered as. Whether it's being a source of love and support for family, being a good friend, or standing up for what you believe in, your legacy will be built from the life you live today.

Understanding your divine design

Discovering your purpose and leaving a meaningful legacy often begins with seeking God's guidance. It's about taking time to ask for clarity and direction in your life, especially when you're unsure of the next steps. Through prayer and quiet reflection, you can find the answers that guide you toward your true purpose.

Seeking Clarity and Direction

Prayer is a powerful way to connect with God and ask for wisdom. It's not just about asking for things you want, but about opening yourself to guidance, clarity, and understanding. When you pray, you are taking time to listen as much as to speak, allowing God to show you the path He has planned for you.

For example, if you feel unsure about what you should do next in life, whether it's related to your career, relationships, or personal growth, prayer can help provide that sense of direction. It's a way to ask God to show you what matters most and to help you focus on the things that truly align with your purpose.

Sometimes, the answers don't come right away, but by continually seeking God's guidance, you will start to feel more at peace with the decisions you need to make. It's important to remember that prayer is not about getting instant answers but about building a relationship with God and trusting that He will guide you in the right direction over time.

Using Journaling to Reflect on Your Thoughts

Journaling is another helpful practice that allows you to process your thoughts and reflect on what you're learning. Writing down your prayers, thoughts, and reflections helps you track your journey, making it easier to see how God is working in your life. When you journal, you can look back and see patterns or recurring ideas that might show you what direction you should be heading in.

After praying for guidance, you might start to notice certain ideas or thoughts coming up repeatedly. By writing them down, you give yourself the chance to explore those thoughts more deeply. Journaling allows you to capture your feelings, your uncertainties, and your hopes, and over time, it can reveal what is truly important to you.

It's a simple practice, but journaling alongside prayer gives you the space to reflect on what God may be trying to show you. It can also help you stay focused on your journey, reminding you of the prayers you've made and the insights you've received.

Quiet Reflection

Meditation is about taking the time to sit in quiet reflection, allowing your mind to settle and opening yourself up to deeper insights. It's a practice of stillness, where you create space in your life to connect with your thoughts, feelings, and, most importantly, your spiritual self. In moments of meditation, you can experience clarity and a sense of peace that helps you feel more connected to God's guidance.

Quiet Reflection: When you meditate, you're giving yourself time to pause from the busyness of life. It's a chance to clear your mind from distractions and focus on the present moment. By creating this quiet space, you allow your thoughts to settle, and in that stillness, insights can begin to emerge. It's in these moments that deeper understanding often surfaces, whether it's about your purpose, the decisions you're facing, or how you can move forward in life.

A day filled with noise and activity, sitting down for a few minutes of quiet reflection can bring a sense of calm. During that time, you might start to feel a clearer sense of what matters most or find answers to the questions you've been carrying in your heart.

Divine Design: Meditation also offers the chance to feel a deeper connection with God. In the stillness, you can feel more attuned to your spiritual side, and this can create a stronger bond with your faith. It's a time when you can listen inwardly and allow God's guidance to become clearer. Meditation isn't about emptying the mind; it's about focusing your heart on the things that really matter and opening yourself up to spiritual guidance.

Taking time to meditate regularly can help you stay grounded, centered, and connected to the bigger picture of your life. It's a simple yet powerful practice that encourages both reflection and spiritual growth.

Focus on your unique Purpose

Living with purpose means aligning your actions and decisions with God's plan for your life. This requires you to prioritize your time, set meaningful goals, and act with intention. By focusing on these areas, you ensure that your daily choices move you closer to fulfilling your purpose.

Prioritize Your Time

It's important to make sure your time is spent on things that reflect your purpose and values. This means being mindful of how you use your time each day. *Are you dedicating time to activities that bring you closer to your goals and to what really matters, or are you caught up in things that don't serve your purpose?* By prioritizing what's important, you can ensure that your efforts are focused where they should be. Time is limited, and being intentional about how you spend it helps you stay on track.

Set Meaningful Goals

Once you have clarity about your purpose, the next step is to set goals that reflect that purpose. These aren't just short-term goals, but goals that align with your long-term vision for your life. Think about what you want to accomplish, not just in terms of career or personal success, but in terms of the impact you want to make. Goals should be driven by the values you hold and the kind of legacy you want to leave. By setting clear and meaningful goals, you create a roadmap that helps you stay connected to your purpose.

Take Intentional Action

Having goals is important, but it's even more important to consistently take action that moves you toward those goals. Every choice and every step should reflect your commitment to fulfilling your purpose. This means making deliberate decisions and being consistent in your actions. Even small actions can lead to big changes when they are focused on the right things. By acting with intention, you ensure that you are not just going through the motions but are actively working toward a life that reflects your purpose and values.

Invest in Relationships

One of the most valuable ways to live a life of purpose is through investing in relationships. The connections you build with others can leave a lasting impact, not just on their lives, but on yours as well. When you focus on meaningful relationships, you create opportunities to guide, support, and serve those around you.

Sharing your wisdom and experience is a powerful way to guide others. Whether it's through formal mentorship or simply offering advice, you can help someone grow in their personal or spiritual life. Mentoring doesn't always mean having all the answers, it's about being there for someone, offering guidance, and helping them navigate their own journey. By mentoring or disciplining someone, you pass on the lessons you've learned and offer support that can inspire and strengthen them.

Relationships thrive when they are built on trust and mutual support. Building meaningful connections means taking the time to develop relationships that are real and deep. This isn't just about casual friendships, but about relationships where you genuinely care for each other and can lean on one another. Whether with family, friends, or colleagues, these connections bring purpose and joy to life. The support you give and receive through these relationships can help you stay grounded and focused on what truly matters.

Serving others is one of the most direct ways to make a positive impact. When you give your time and energy to helping those around you, you're not only improving their lives but also living out your purpose. Whether it's volunteering, helping a neighbor, or simply being there for someone in need, serving others shows compassion and commitment to making the world a better place. By serving those around you, you build stronger connections and lead by example, showing others the value of caring for one another.

Leave a Lasting Impact

Leaving a lasting impact means ensuring that the lessons, values, and experiences you've gained in life continue to benefit others long after you're gone. By sharing your story, living in a way that reflects your faith, and inspiring others to live with intention, you can create a legacy that endures.

Share Your Story and Wisdom

The experiences and lessons you've gathered throughout your life are incredibly valuable. Sharing them can help younger people or those looking for guidance. It's not about being perfect or knowing everything, but offering what you've learned in a way that's honest and helpful. Talking about your journey, whether it's the struggles, the victories, or the lessons in between, can give others perspective and help them find their own way.

Imagine someone who's been through a lot, like a parent who worked hard to build a stable life for their family. Instead of keeping their journey private, they share stories with their children about the challenges they faced, whether it was juggling work and family or making tough decisions. They don't sugarcoat it, but they also share what helped them get through those times, like staying patient, being kind to others, or trusting in the process.

One day, their son or daughter might face a difficult situation and remember something their parent told them, a piece of advice that sticks because it came from real experience. Maybe it helps them make a better decision or just feel less alone during a tough moment. By sharing their story, the parent is not someone telling tales, they're giving their children something real to hold on to.

> *Passing down your wisdom can guide others, giving them the tools to face their own challenges with more confidence and understanding.*

Your values and actions

Honoring God through your actions is about living in a way that reflects your faith, not through perfection, but by being true to your values. It's about showing kindness, honesty, and generosity in everyday life. These small actions can leave a lasting impact on the people around you and show what truly matters to you. Living this way isn't about grand gestures but about making thoughtful choices that align with your beliefs and reflect your connection with God.

For example, think of someone who is known for always being kind, with family, friends, or even strangers. Their actions come from a place of faith and wanting to do what's right, not for recognition, but because it's who they are. Over time, people around them notice this consistency, and it leaves an impression. They see someone who lives with integrity, who tries to do good, and who handles challenges with grace and patience.

A simple story could be a father who, despite having a tough job and facing personal challenges, always made time to help others. He was known for stepping in when people needed a hand, helping a neighbor fix a broken chair, or offering advice to someone going through a hard time. His family saw this and learned from his actions, not because he talked about faith all the time, but because he showed it in how he lived. When his children grew up, they remembered those small moments of kindness and service, and they wanted to live the same way.

> *These small, consistent actions become your legacy, showing people around you what it means to live with purpose and faith.*

Inspire Others to Live Intentionally

Living with purpose and intention doesn't just change your life, it inspires others too. When people see you living out your values, staying focused on what truly matters, and making thoughtful choices, they begin to reflect on their own lives. It encourages them to think about their own passions, purpose, and what they want to achieve.

You don't have to say much or do something big to inspire others. Sometimes, just the way you live your everyday life can influence those around you. Your actions, how you treat others, and the decisions you make, can serve as an example. People notice when someone lives with intention and focus, and it can motivate them to do the same in their own lives.

A mother who is deeply committed to helping her community. She doesn't just talk about it; she spends her time volunteering, organizing events, and being there for those in need. Her children watch her and learn from what she does. Without her even telling them to, they start getting involved, finding ways to help others because they've been inspired by her actions. This shows how living with purpose can inspire others to follow a similar path.

> *The way you live can have a ripple effect, where others take what they've learned from you and pass it on, creating a cycle of positive influence.*

Legacy Types

Soulful Legacy

A spiritual legacy is about living in a way that reflects your faith and values and passing these on to others. It's not just about what you say but how you live each day. Your actions, kindness, and the choices you make show others what you believe and how your faith shapes your life.

When you live out your faith, people around you can see how it gives you strength, direction, and meaning. By being open about your own journey—how your beliefs have guided you through hard times and brought joy and peace—you help others understand the value of living by strong principles.

A spiritual legacy also involves encouraging those around you to find their own faith or to hold onto values that matter. You do this by leading through example, offering guidance when needed, and showing how faith can positively impact life. It's not about preaching, but about quietly living in a way that inspires others.

Relational Legacy

A relational legacy is all about the connections you build with the people closest to you, your family, friends, and community. It's about how you treat them, the bonds you create, and the love and support you give over the years. When you focus on building meaningful relationships, you leave behind something that lasts longer than any material possessions: the memories and trust you built with others.

Being present for those who matter most is key to building a relational legacy. This means spending time with family, checking in on friends, and being there for those in your community when they need you. These small moments of care and attention show people that you value and appreciate them. Over time, these connections deepen, and the love and support you've given becomes something they remember long after you're gone.

A relational legacy isn't about grand gestures but about consistently showing up for people. It's about making sure that the relationships in your life are built on a foundation of trust and respect. By treating others with kindness, listening when they need to talk, and offering support when they're struggling, you build a bond that stands the test of time.

When people look back at your life, they'll remember the way you made them feel, the conversations you shared, and the times you were there when they needed someone.

Professional Legacy

A professional legacy is about the lasting impact you leave through your work and service. It's about achieving success in your career and how you contributed to your field and the positive changes you helped create. Your professional legacy is built on the projects you completed, the people you mentored, and the values you upheld in your workplace.

When you dedicate yourself to making a difference in your work, you create something meaningful that lasts beyond your time there. It might be through the innovations you introduced, the improvements you brought to processes, or simply the way you treated your colleagues. By working with purpose and integrity, you leave behind a legacy that reflects your commitment to doing something that matters.

Mentorship is a key part of a professional legacy. Guiding others and helping them grow in their careers ensures that the knowledge and skills you've developed are passed on to the next generation. The people you've mentored will carry forward the lessons and values you've shared, continuing the positive impact long after you've moved on.

Leaving a professional legacy also means standing for something beyond personal achievement.

Corporate Legacy

A business legacy that goes beyond profit is one that prioritizes making a positive impact on the world. This type of legacy is built on a foundation of purpose, values, and a commitment to creating long-term value for all stakeholders. One company that has built a legacy of environmental sustainability is an outdoor apparel manufacturer that has made a commitment to using only sustainable materials in its products. This company has also implemented a number of initiatives aimed at reducing its environmental impact, including using renewable energy sources, reducing water usage, and implementing a recycling program. By prioritizing environmental sustainability, this company has created a legacy that inspires and motivates others to take action to protect the environment.

A business legacy that goes beyond profit is not just about what a company does, but also about how it does it. It's about creating a culture of purpose, values, and accountability that permeates every aspect of the business. Another company that has built a legacy of social impact is an eyewear manufacturer that has made a commitment to providing vision care to people in need. This company has implemented a number of initiatives aimed at providing access to vision care, including partnering with non-profit organizations to provide free eye exams and glasses to people in need. The company has also implemented a number of sustainability initiatives, including using recycled materials in its products and reducing its carbon footprint. By prioritizing social impact and sustainability, this company has created a legacy that truly makes a difference in the world.

Personal Legacy

A personal legacy is about the kind of person you were, how you treated others, and the values you lived by. It's not just about what you did in life but how you made others feel and the principles you stood for. People will remember you for your character, integrity, and the wisdom you shared with them.

Being known for your kindness, honesty, and fairness is a big part of leaving a personal legacy. The way you care for and support others, whether through big acts or small moments, makes a lasting impression. People will remember how you treated them with respect and understanding, even in difficult situations.

Integrity is another important part of your personal legacy. Being true to your word, doing what's right, and standing by your values show others that you can be trusted. People will remember the consistency between what you believed and how you lived.

Wisdom is the knowledge and life lessons you pass on to others. As you go through life, you learn things that can help others, whether through advice, guidance or simply setting a good example. Sharing your experiences and the lessons you've learned helps shape the lives of those around you.

> *"The greatest legacy we can leave is the impact we have on others."*

By accepting the unique purpose that God has given you, you are not only living a meaningful life but also setting the foundation for a legacy that will continue to inspire others. When you align your actions with this purpose, you create a lasting impact that touches the lives of those around you. Every action, every choice you make, becomes part of this greater purpose.

Living with this kind of intentionality means that you are consciously choosing to live in a way that reflects love, kindness, and the values you hold dear. When others see how you live with purpose, they are often inspired to reflect on their own lives and make changes that bring them closer to their own purpose. Your life becomes an example of how living with meaning and love can transform not only your own path but the paths of others.

A life lived with purpose also glorifies God by showing others the beauty of living according to His plan. When you accept your purpose, you are fulfilling the role He has for you, and that brings honor to Him. The way you live your life can be a reflection of His love and grace, serving as a reminder to others of the power of faith and the peace that comes from living in line with His will.

This type of living brings deep fulfillment. When you know that you are living out the purpose you were created for, there is a sense of peace and joy that comes with it.

As I sit in silence surrounded by the quite stillness of the early morning hours near Heathrow. I want to leave you with a sense of hope, optimism, and empowerment. Remember, your purpose is a unique and precious gift, woven into the very fabric of your being. Don't be afraid to unravel the threads of your passions, values, and strengths to discover the beautiful tapestry that is your life's work. As you embark on this adventure, I offer you a blessing: May you be guided by the whispers of your heart, may you be strengthened by the resilience of your spirit, and may you be illuminated by the light of your highest potential. And when the journey gets tough, as it sometimes will, remember that you are not alone. In the AI driven world you are part of a global community of purpose pursuing individuals who are rising to make a difference in the world. No matter what challenges AI brings keep shining your light and know that it will inspire others to do the same. Together, let's create a world that is more compassionate, equitable, and just - a world that reflects the beauty, diversity, and wonder of the God given human spirit.

Conclusion

How does living with purpose help combat loneliness and build meaningful connections? When you live with intention and align your actions with your values, you create deeper relationships that nurture both yourself and others. These relationships form a strong foundation for community, as purposeful living naturally fosters connection. Your legacy is a reflection of how you live your life, and by living with purpose, you create a lasting impact that extends beyond your own experiences. Through purposeful connections, you can transcend isolation and leave behind a meaningful legacy.

Reflective Questions

Here are some questions to help you think about the role of purpose in your relationships and how it shapes your legacy:

- *How has loneliness affected you, and what types of connections can you make to bring more purpose into your life?*
- *Can you share experiences where meaningful relationships helped you discover or nurture your purpose?*

- *When you imagine your legacy, what impact do you hope to leave on the people and the world around you?*
- *How can you build relationships with intention, focusing on purpose and mutual support?*
- *How does having a sense of purpose help you overcome feelings of loneliness?*

Practical Applications

Practicing self-compassion and mindfulness can help you connect with yourself, laying the groundwork for building meaningful relationships with others. Engaging in community service is another powerful way to create connections and find purpose through helping others. Reflecting on your personal values will guide you toward relationships that align with your goals and purpose. Focus on nurturing meaningful relationships, and consider writing a personal legacy statement to clarify the impact you want to have on the world.

Actionable Steps

Make volunteering a regular part of your routine to build connections and serve others. Join a community group that shares your values or interests, helping you grow your network of purposeful relationships. Set up monthly check-ins with friends and loved ones to maintain and deepen these important connections.

Principles

1. *Purpose combats loneliness.*
2. *Meaningful connections nurture purpose.*
3. *Legacy reflects purposeful living.*
4. *Intentional relationships foster community.*
5. *Purposeful living transcends isolation.*
6. *Lasting impact results from purpose-driven legacy.*

Questions

1. *How has loneliness impacted your life, and what purpose-driven connections can help?*
2. *Share experiences of meaningful relationships that nurtured your purpose.*
3. *Imagine your legacy; what impact do you want to leave?*
4. *How can you cultivate intentional relationships?*
5. *What role does purpose play in overcoming loneliness?*

Actionable Steps

1. *Practice self-compassion and mindfulness.*
2. *Engage in community service.*
3. *Reflect on personal values.*
4. *Develop meaningful relationships.*
5. *Write a personal legacy statement.*

About the Book

What is your purpose?

To find clarity in a world full of distractions?

It's about understanding what truly drives you and how to live a life that feels meaningful. Through reflections on values, relationships, and your place in the world, this journey will guide you toward discovering what really matters. It's not about grand achievements but about the small choices you make every day. By exploring your God-given purpose, you'll find ways to live more intentionally and create a lasting impact. Let this book remind you of what makes your life meaningful and unique. Read this exciting book to find out:

- What empowers youth to overcome addictions and gives sense of identity and meaning.
- What promotes understanding of gender roles and resolves false feminism and toxic masculinity.
- What counters extremism and terrorism by fostering inclusive and constructive approach.

- What transcends racial and caste-based divisions and celebrates unique value, worth of every individual.
- What provides sense of identity, meaning and direction enabling individuals to navigate uncertainties posed by Artificial intelligence.
- Why AI singularity and digital sentience cannot change foundational human Purpose.

About the Author

Santhosh Asir is an IT professional with over 20 years of experience, holding degrees in Engineering from Bharathiar University and a Master's from BITS Pilani. His career has taken him across the globe, including Argentina, China, Germany, Netherlands, Qatar, and the United Kingdom, where he currently works in senior management for a leading airline.

As a Certified Solution Architect in cloud technology and trained in generative AI, Santhosh is a visionary author, dynamic speaker and passionate change agent who is dedicated in catalyzing personal and societal transformation. Offering a unique blend of spiritual insight, practical wisdom and visionary leadership. He wrote this book to ignite a spark within readers to awaken them to the transformative power of purpose, passion, legacy and empower them to live a life that truly matters.

Santhosh lives in West London with his wife Sujitha and their two children, Shannon and Shiphra. Through his writing, he hopes to inspire others, especially the younger generation, to explore their own values and purpose in life.

For more information:
www.purposerenaissance.com

www.ingramcontent.com/pod-product-compliance
Lightning Source LLC
LaVergne TN
LVHW041216150826
845673LV00001B/420

9798896328384